The Write Track

THE WRITE TRACK

How to Succeed as a
Freelance Writer in Canada

Second Edition,
Revised and Expanded

Betty Jane Wylie

THE DUNDURN GROUP
TORONTO · OXFORD

Proofreader: Jennifer Bergeron
Design: Jennifer Scott
Printer: University of Toronto Press

National Library of Canada Cataloguing in Publication Data

Wylie, Betty Jane, 1931-
    The write track : how to succeed as a freelance writer in Canada / Betty Jane Wylie. — 2nd ed., rev. and expanded

ISBN 1-55002-444-2

1. Authorship — Vocational guidance — Canada. I. Title.

PN153.W95 2003   808'.02'02371   C2003-900343-4

1   2   3   4   5   07   06   05   04   03

  Canadä

THE CANADA COUNCIL | LE CONSEIL DES ARTS
FOR THE ARTS | DU CANADA
SINCE 1957 DEPUIS 1957

ONTARIO ARTS COUNCIL
CONSEIL DES ARTS DE L'ONTARIO

We acknowledge the support of the **Canada Council for the Arts** and the **Ontario Arts Council** for our publishing program. We also acknowledge the financial support of the **Government of Canada** through the **Book Publishing Industry Development Program** and **The Association for the Export of Canadian Books,** and the **Government of Ontario** through the **Ontario Book Publishers Tax Credit** program, and the **Ontario Media Development Corporation's Ontario Book Initiative.**

Care has been taken to trace the ownership of copyright material used in this book. The author and the publisher welcome any information enabling them to rectify any references or credit in subsequent editions.

J. Kirk Howard, President

Printed and bound in Canada.⊕
Printed on recycled paper.
www.dundurn.com

Dundurn Press
8 Market Street
Suite 200
Toronto, Ontario, Canada
M5E 1M6

Dundurn Press
73 Lime Walk
Headington, Oxford,
England
OX3 7AD

Dundurn Press
2250 Military Road
Tonawanda NY
U.S.A. 14150

To Donald Martin, mentor and friend

Acknowledgements

A new edition always involves new acknowledgements, especially when a new publisher is involved as well. It's a honeymoon, so far, and I'm grateful to Dundurn Press for having the wisdom to shepherd this book back into print — for the readers' sake, not mine. It contains the best advice I can give you and I am grateful to all the people who have taught me my lessons, for good or ill.

Uppermost in my mind are the new people on the publishing scene who have been so helpful with the updating of information, specifically, Susan Stevenson, Executive Director of the Periodical Writers' Association of Canada; Deborah Windsor, Executive Director, and Siobhan O'Connor, Assistant Director, of The Writers' Union of Canada; and Cindy Goldrick, Manager, Membership and Communications, of Access Copyright, the wonderful new fairy godmother that is going to make us all rich, or at least recognized and appreciated when our words are bandied about. As for Marian Hebb, whom I have dubbed the patron saint of writers, her legal assistance and moral support have been invaluable.

Thank you, and enjoy!

Published and Produced Work
by Betty Jane Wylie

Non-Fiction
Letters to Icelanders: Exploring the Northern Soul
Enough: Lifestyle and Financial Planning for Simpler Living
Family: An Exploration
Beginnings: A Book for Widows (20th anniversary edition)
The Best Is Yet to Come (with Christopher Cottier)
Life's Losses (reprint of New Beginnings)
Everywoman's Money Book (with Lynne Macfarlane)
New Beginnings: Living Through Loss and Grief
All in the Family: A Survival Guide for Living and Loving in a Changing World
Successfully Single

Cookbooks
Solo Chef: Recipes, Tips, Advice and Encouragement for Single Cooks
The Betty Jane Wylie Cheese Cookbook
Encore: The Leftovers Cookbook

Poetry
The Better Half: Women's Voices
Something Might Happen
The Second Shepherds' Play (one version)

Belles Lettres
Reading Between the Lines: The Diaries of Women
Men! A Collection of Quotations About Men by Women

Biography
The Book of Matthew
The Horsburgh Scandal

Inspirational
Betty Jane's Diary: Lessons Children Taught Me
Betty Jane's Diary: Passages
Betty Jane's Diary: Holidays and Celebrations
No Two Alike

Children's Books
John of a Thousand Faces
Tecumseh

Plays
Veranda
Time Bomb
Double Vision
A Place on Earth
The Horsburgh Scandal (with Theatre Passe Muraille)
 Mark
Jason
Androgyne
Angel
Speculum
Grace Under Pressure
The Second Shepherds' Play (two translations, one adaptation; see Musicals)
Steps
How to Speak Male
Help Is on the Way (six-part series)
A Day In the Life (two short plays, one theme)
Double Swap (with Michael Cole)
Size Ten
I See You
An Enemy of the People (adaptation)

Plays for Children
Don't Just Stand There — Jiggle! (a collection of puppet plays)
Kingsayer
The Old Woman and the Pedlar

Radio Plays

Memories of Canada
How to Speak Male
Sybil: A Novel for Radio
Mountain Woman
Victorian Spice (award winner)
Betty Jane's Diary (a daily personal column syndicated by Berkeley Studio, Toronto, broadcast by independent radio stations in Canada)

Musicals

Beowulf (music by Victor Davies)
Soap Bubbles (music by Victor Davies)
The Second Shepherds' Play (church version, music by Quenten Doolittle)
Boy in a Cage (chamber opera, music by Ken Nichols)

Recordings

Beowulf (three-record album, Golden Toad Label)
Beowulf (two-record album, Daffodil Label)

Television

Women, Lifestyle, and Money (thirteen-part series, writer/narrator/host)
Coming of Age (Movie of the Week, with Donald Martin)
CrossTalk (twelve-part series for VISION TV, writer, facilitator, host)
Shadow Lake (Movie of the Week, story credit)

Journalism

Published in Canadian magazines and newspapers, including:
Maclean's, Chatelaine, Homemakers, Toronto Life, Miss Chatelaine (now *Flare*), *Calgary Magazine, Canadian Living, Performing Arts, Canadian Theatre Review, Recipes Only, Fiddlehead, Forum, Fifty Plus, Gourmet* (U.S.A.), *Today, The Canadian, The Icelandic Canadian, Prairie Fire, Quest, City Woman, City Magazine, Ontario Living, Leisureways* (now *Journey*), the *Globe and Mail*, the *Toronto Star*, the *Winnipeg Free Press*, and the *Boston Globe*.

Special Newspaper Assignments

"The Old Lady Caper" and "The Psycho Trip" (two, five-part series of investigative journalism)
"Summer Soap" (three-month daily summer serial)

Books About Her Work

Female Parts: The Art and Politics of Female Playwrights, by Yvonne Hodkinson
The Canadian Dramatist, Volume Two, by Diane Bessai

Anthologies Where Her Work Has Appeared

Dropped Threads: What We Aren't Told ("The Imaginary Woman")
Inter S E C T I O N S: Fiction and Poetry from the Banff Centre for the Arts ("Mirror Image", excerpt from an unpublished novel)
Going Some Place ("A Guest of Karen Blixen")
Six Fantasy Plays for Children ("The Old Woman and the Pedlar")
Unexpected Fictions ("Memories of Chocolate Sauce")
Recipes Only
First Class Acts ("The Discovery Trunk")
The Perfect Piece ("Anna")
Another Perfect Piece ("Jason")

Table of Contents

PART ONE

In the Beginning

In Which the Writer Explains How the Oldest Living Canadian Full-time Freelancer Got Her Start

"Are you working or are you writing?" the reporter asked me, curious about something I had written. I told her I didn't think the two activities were mutually exclusive. Her question came at the beginning of my freelance career, clearly showing the basic misconception people have about writing and writers, even those who are in the field. It is generally assumed that writing is something you do in your spare time, when the mood or the muse hits you, preferably with suitable background music, and someone preparing good food and drink for you when you are through. It seems to be a glamorous profession, both dilettante and fulfilling, portable and profitable. An aura surrounds a writer, or the idea of Writer, a mystique that more practical and prosperous people envy.

But writing is work. Anyone who has attempted to write seriously, and even those who try simply to write — not art but business reports, minutes, summaries, and such — know that it is work, that trying to squeeze words from the head onto paper in a coherent form is very hard work. And when you decide to make writing your day job, what can have possessed you? Not the muse. She may have tripped you, but you're the one who put your head in the snare. Because what you must realize when you make this decision is that you have suddenly become a small-business entrepreneur as well as a writer. It may sound oxymoronic to others to call yourself a working writer but you are in the business of selling your words, or you want to be if you're reading this book. Call yourself, as someone once called me, a professional communicator. Professional means you get paid; communicate means to:

- exchange information or signals by talk, writing, gesture, etc.;
- pass along; transmit;
- get in touch with; get through to;
- be connected; and
- receive Holy Communion.
  (*The Gage Canadian Dictionary*)

The first four are not givens, because you have to work at them, but they are possible through human effort. You may achieve the last one if you are blessed. I haven't met a writer who hasn't at one time or another felt the words flow from somewhere other than the brain right onto the paper. That can only be called a blessing.

So what if that puts you in the category of mystic? Accept it and be grateful. Just don't forget that if you intend to make a living as a word swami you have to be a hustler as well. Be prepared to spend at least 30 percent of your time doing business, more when starting out or in a dry spell, that is, between paying assignments/gigs. Consider this time as an essential part of your work. Don't ever imagine that once you quit your day job you'll never have to do drudge again, that you will do nothing but write. Some day you may be able to afford a clone; until then, you're it.

If you do quit your day job, you think it would be nice to make a decent living as a writer. Define decent. The Canadian Conference of the Arts estimated the average earnings of artists and creators in 1995 at "just over $18,000 a year, less than taxi drivers, hotel clerks and hairstylists" — and they get tips! CCA concluded that "artists and creators are among the most highly educated but least well paid workers in Canada." I/you could have told them that. And yet you remain undaunted and hopeful that you will be able to produce a realistic living wage for various writing services rendered and enjoy your life on the way by. It takes a lot of something (courage, blind faith, foolhardiness, chutzpah, a trust fund?) to fly in the face of such statistics. You will find, as I did, when you decide to live by your words and wonder if your words are good enough, that you will often quote these words of Samuel Johnson:

> *Depend upon it, sir, knowing you're going to be hanged in*
> *a fortnight concentrates the mind wonderfully.*

I often quote them to others, too — to laypeople who ask me about Writer's Block and who wonder whether I ever want to give up. Freelance writers can seldom afford Writer's Block and they certainly can't afford to give up. What they need is a little craft. Craft is what I am offering, street smarts and survival tips that I have learned over the years. I will share both the long-term approach and the nitty-gritty assaults, pointing out mountains to climb or go around and the mole-hills to trip on or step over.

GETTING STARTED

I don't remember not writing. I wrote my first short story when I was five and my first poem when I was seven. I managed to persuade my father to let me take a liberal arts course, heavy on languages, rather than following in his footsteps with science and medicine. I took a B.A. double honours in French and English and a master's degree in English (majoring in twentieth-century poetry, with a minor in Anglo-Saxon and Old Norse), both from the University of Manitoba because by that time I was engaged to Bill Wylie and didn't want to leave him. I married seventeen days after I graduated. We did that in those days.

I still wanted to write, but time eluded me while I put in a long apprenticeship doing other things, like having (four) children and becoming a very good cook. I wrote in my spare time, which was not very spare. I had planned to increase my writing time when my last child entered school but was foiled in my perfect plan because my last child was brain-damaged. He didn't enter school at the usual age and required time-consuming homework: special training and help from his mother.

I began to write for money when my older daughter needed ortho-dontic work — short talk pieces for the CBC — and to perform on tel-evision talking about early Winnipeg history, which I had begun to research for a novel I had in mind. I managed to write the first draft of the novel, which was rejected, and a few plays, which were not. Turned out I liked dialogue better than description. I wrote puppet plays as a community service for the Junior League of Winnipeg puppetry troupe and became script consultant to the Puppeteers of America, giving puppet-playwriting workshops at the annual festival. There was no payment for these services, or for the productions of my puppet plays by other League troupes in North America.

In 1967, I wrote a Canadian version of Ibsen's *An Enemy of the People,* which was produced on the main stage of the Manitoba Theatre Centre. This brought both the Wylies to the MTC's attention and my husband was invited to join the board. He found his true vocation, taking over the theatre shortly after as general manager and moving on to the Stratford Festival within four years. I had spent more time painting the big old house in Winnipeg we had moved into than writing, but found time to write another play, for children but with live actors, produced at MTC in 1968, the fall before we moved to Stratford. While we were there, I had a new short play in a studio series picked up by CBC Radio; another version of *An Enemy of the People* (1972) commissioned by the St. Lawrence Centre in Toronto, which toured the National Arts Centre in Ottawa; and a new full-length drama produced at the new Third Stage (now the Tom Patterson Theatre) in Stratford. All this activity, though remunerated, was not for money but for love. I spent more time cooking than writing, as we entertained guests all summer during the Stratford Festival season.

In the late winter of 1973 I had an encouraging reader's report from a publisher about my novel, with the invitation to get back to them with a new draft. I found the letter last year. Unfortunately, I didn't follow up on it because in the spring of 1973 my husband suddenly died. Apart from my staggering grief, I was terrified. I had no idea how I was going to live, let alone support myself and my children, then aged twelve, fourteen, sixteen, and eighteen, the oldest off to university that first fall, the youngest still requiring enormous amounts of time and money.

Insurance paid off the house and bought me some modest investments that provided (very) modest help, supplemented by the relatively new Widow's Allowance. I considered finding work at a university because I had marked essays for ten years in Winnipeg after I married, but tenure tracks and closed shops being what they were, I couldn't get my foot in a door in an Ontario university; the closest ones were too distant from Stratford, anyway. I could write plays, but as playwright Bernard Slade (*Same Time Next Year*) said, "You can make a killing in the theatre, but not a living." I needed money, fast.

For one summer between university degrees, I had worked at the *Winnipeg Free Press* on the Women's Page (now called Life or Focus, used to be Society). The Women's Page at the *Stratford Beacon Herald* was open, but very poorly paid for long hours, including some night work. My lawyer suggested I might do better by freelancing. Why not try it for six months? So I did.

My start was more dramatic and forced than most and I tell you this because you must assess your own resources with a steely eye before you leave your day job. I was thrust into my "choice" to freelance. I had no other viable alternatives and I was working without much of a safety net. Other writers have made more reasoned, controlled moves, buoyed up by a book contract or a windfall. You will be wise and also fortunate to have enough of a cushion to be able to buy shelter, food, and paper, plus disks and printer cartridges.

The late American writer John Gardner had one practical suggestion to offer a struggling writer: "Living off one's spouse or lover is an excellent survival tactic." Male or female, you must carefully evaluate all your assets, including your mate, if you have one.

Not having a mate, I had a different game plan. What I hoped to do was to write non-fiction in order to support both my children and my habit, my habit being playwriting. I was going to pretend to be a journalist, a reporter, an essayist, whatever, and keep on trying to be a playwright with my spare time and energy. Once, when I had complained to my husband how long I spent with the iron (in those days before permanent press) when I had a pressing engagement I would rather keep with my typewriter, he gave me what I called my Wylie Grant for Ironing, to buy me more time to write. Now I intended to subsidize myself with another kind of Wylie Grant (Lord, *grant* me my wits). Thus, my goal was to be a professional journalist, writing for money; my purpose was to be a playwright.

Your goal, too, will be something like mine: short-term, some kind of survival. Your purpose, also like mine, will be long-term — your aim in life. What do you as a writer hope to do: entertain, amuse, instruct, move, teach, touch others? The question is, why? Why do you want to knock out your brains and heart trying to be a writer? The best answer is, because. Not because of the money, certainly. Haven't we already established that? There's more to it than money. (I'll get to the passion in more detail later, the stuff that makes you stick.) Because you need to communicate. Because it's what you do, it's who you are. Because you realize that your goals and purpose are one and the same and you and they are all of a piece. Because it just comes naturally, and if it doesn't all the time, it will if you do it all the time. You know the story about Saint Francis of Assisi, who was hoeing onions one day when someone (a reporter?) came and asked him what he would do if he knew the world was going to end by evening. The saint answered calmly, "Finish hoeing the onions."

Maybe you should give yourself a more practical end-of-the-world test. This question is right out of a business-motivation book but it can be applied in an artistic context. Ask yourself where you want to be and what you want to be doing in six months, one year, five years. Write down the answers if you like. Then, just as if you were working on business goals, because you are, analyze all your activities to see whether or not they contribute to your purpose. Label your tasks A, B, or C, in order of importance — that is, in terms of their priorities and usefulness in accomplishing your purpose. When you've done that, it's a simple (?) matter of selecting and arranging your daily work and activities according to this master plan. I do this so automatically now that it's second nature. I am addicted to lists, and this kind of list reassures me. I plan the next day with a list, as well as each month, which I see as a block of usable writing time, and, of course, each new year.

Once you decide to quit your day job to make time for writing, the amount of time suddenly at your disposal is terrifying. If you've become accustomed to snatching time wherever you could steal it, staying up too late or getting up ridiculously early or skipping your weekend chores, the hours now stretching ahead of you may seem endless and heady at first. It seemed that way to me, especially, I think, because suddenly I no longer had someone coming home every night to spend/steal delicious hours with. I was kept to some kind of a routine by the presence of my children, and I still had to prepare meals, wash clothes, shop for groceries, and so on, but even so, I remember realizing that I had all the time in the world. I was not that tempted to goof off because one, I needed money, and two, my writing gave me some focus and meaning when I thought my life had very little.

You leave dull routine behind when you decide to court the muse of creation. Like me, you will find that your courtship must be both assiduous and faithful if you're going to win the creature. My father used to comment after a vacation that he had to court the Muse of Work to get himself back into a working mode. That's our muse, the Working One, the one we want to woo and keep. Forget Melpomene and her sister muses.

But don't forget that while you are looking out for Number One, you must also be looking out for Number Two — your reader(s). You are, after all, in the business of communicating. To communicate you must close the connection between you and your receiver. Holy Communion, Batman, let's get on with it!

PART TWO

The Write Stuff

*In Which the Writer Tells Us
What Makes a Writer*

THE ITCH

Wannabe writers are always asking "real" — that is, published — writers or writing teachers or professionals in the field if they have what it takes to be a writer. The insecurity about their qualifications is matched only by the driving force that makes them write. In my own case, I think I have discovered what it is that makes me keep writing in spite of all the setbacks, terrors, obstacles, hazards, and disappointments hurled into my path: failure goes to my head.

When a red flag is waved at me — red as in stop, red as in quit while you're ahead, red as in Go back! Go back! — I do not go back. I snort and paw the ground, take a deep breath, gather up all my stubborn resources, and charge again. Once more into the fray. How humble I could be were I successful, graciously accepting accolades, (faintly) demurring at praise heaped upon me, lightly wearing my laurels, but I have not yet achieved such generosity of spirit. The more I am rejected and ignored, the more defiant I become, and the more belligerent about proving my worth. I have to be, because no one else is. This obstinacy in the face of rejection characterizes a writer almost as much as a passion for words. Laypeople call this arrogance. They're wrong. It's self-preservation and it throws up a protective barrier around the deepest longing in a writer's soul.

I suppose if you or I could quit, we would, maybe. A lot of people do, and probably make more money doing other things. But those who are hooked can't. I always had this feeling that I derived my strength from the keys of my typewriter and I did literally get sick when deprived of them for too long. It doesn't matter whether you tap the keys of something's keyboard or curl your fingers lovingly around a pencil, Bic or Mont Blanc, the addictive activity is the same: pushing words from your head through your hands onto paper. If you are a driven being, you can't change. I think I love paper, but it's words I am besotted with. You must feel the same way. People like you and me will never stop writing or thinking about it: practising, stretching, studying, reaching out for new ideas, techniques, and insights, and dancing around with words.

I've heard it said that a passion for art or music manifests itself early in a child, earlier than the love of words and verbal or written expression. I'm not sure I agree with this. It's just that it's harder to recognize a lust for language and an eagerness for expression when everyone around you speaks and most people you know can read, if only functionally and not for the encompassing pleasure we wordmongers constantly pursue. Words are public domain; they belong to everyone as an esoteric knowledge of colour and texture and light or of musical sounds and silence does not.

You simply want to write. Note the difference: real writers want to write, not be a writer. You have long since discovered that you are an addict: you need the fix, the heady feeling of putting words together to create images, emotions, ideas — that, too — but also the joy of fooling around with phrases, dabbling with diction, puttering with punctuation.

> The poet W.H. Auden once offered a clue to identifying
> a real poet: someone who likes "hanging around words
> listening to what they have to say."

Once you've acknowledged this yearning, you must admit you have another desire: to communicate what you have expressed — that is, to find an audience, to be public, to be published. Add one more small wish: You would like your words to be saleable, to be remunerated, not only for the money but for the fact of being considered worth the money. The recognition of the marketplace justifies your own faith in your words, suggests that you have something worth saying, worth listening to/reading. This monetary recognition, however modest the payment may be, bolsters your courage as well, gives you some assurance that you are not an utter fool for wanting to lay your wares in front of total strangers. You are performing an act of communication — reaching people.

It's an ego thing but it's one of the mildest appetites, far less lethal than most, not even hubris, just a small vanity. You can live without it, have, in fact. But while we're talking small vanities and modest rewards, don't forget this. You may not dine with presidents; they may never know how to spell your name in New Guinea (Buster Keaton's definition of fame); crazy people may never think they're you (as Napoleon and Joan of Arc and Hitler and Jesus have been honoured). You can accept that. But once in a while someone will approach you across a crowded airport lounge, or find you in a fast food place (eating chicken with your bare hands), or catch you in a bookstore (putting your book in a more prominent position) and *recognize you*. And sometimes a clerk in that bookstore will know your name when you hand him your credit card. And sometimes a reader will write and tell you how much your words have meant to her. That's what keeps you going. It means that you do have the gift to communicate. Use it well.

THE TALENT

First let's get it clear, the distinction between talent and skill. Talent is natural ability; skill is ability honed by practice, that is, expertise. The parable about the talents was really referring to units of money and illustrated the uselessness of holes in the ground as a place to store money because it doesn't accrue. The Preacher was telling His listeners to use their talents, to invest them and make them grow. At the end of the day, or life, it's not enough to reveal one's talents and take pride that they are still intact. The point is that you're supposed to make the most of what you've been given. Staying with the money idea, we know in any case that merely holding on to money isn't worth much; talents, like dollars, lose their purchasing power. You have to make them real. So with ability. Talent muscles atrophy without massage, toning, and regular exercise.

It's likely that in addition to fooling around with words you enjoy playing with ideas. If you're going to write, this is essential. The question is, do you have something to say? The corollary is, can you think?

I was fifteen when I entered university and began to think. My brother, older and smarter than I, warned me that all I had going for me was a good memory and that when I had to think I'd be in deep trouble. So there I was in first year, working on my first literary essay about Electra in the eponymous play by Euripides, trying to prove my brother wrong by doing my own thinking about some mythological Greek lady without resorting to an academic critique. I got an A+ and learned something worth more than that: Writing is not only putting well-chosen words onto paper in a felicitous order; it should also have meaning.

I remember one of my professors saying that the most mellifluous phrase in the English language was "cellar door" but that the meaning ruined the sound. So a page full of cellar doors isn't going to do much for anyone. You need, in addition to the sound, some reason for using it, and some reasoning behind it. You need, in short, to think.

Anyway, here you are, with a basketful of words and lots of ideas. What are you going to do with them? Do you have the skills to put them all together into thoughtful, saleable forms? Start with a clear-eyed inventory of your talents. Assess the talents you have, the abilities you can hone, and the intelligence you can exercise.

THE SKILLS

> FAMOUS SCENE: *Dinner Party, late 1970s*
> BRAIN SURGEON: *So you're a writer, eh? I've always thought I'd write a book when I retire.*
> FAMOUS CANADIAN AUTHOR: *Really? When I retire, I'm going to try brain surgery.*

Understand this: God gave you talents, not skills (see that parable). You were born with a love of words and a certain talent for using them. Talent is gratuitous; skill is hard-won. Skill is what you do with your talent. Sad to say, all the skill in the world won't make up for a lack of talent or lust for words. The good news is that not many readers or critics will notice the difference unless they are sensitive, astute, and possess certain skills themselves. Usually it takes a century or so for truth/art to come clear, but of course time doesn't allow for a future judgment on talent without skill. (If you become a best-selling writer of schlock with six-figure advances and movie options, it's possible you won't care.) Although the uneven distribution of talent might be a harsh fact of life — nobody ever said it was fair that some people are born with an ear for dialogue or a silver tongue or a nose for news while others are not — it's part of the hand we're dealt when we're born. Almost anyone can shuffle cards; few can palm one unseen without considerable practice. Word skills can be acquired. So can a larger vocabulary, good spelling, and good grammar, as well as a grasp of sentence structure, syntax, phrasing, rhythms, and balance. We stand on the last bastion of rhetoric. We must defend it with all our might — and skill.

Other acquired skills include technique, style, polish, care, accuracy, and power. (There are exercises in writing books: WRITE POWER VERBS! USE TELLING ADJECTIVES!) A close attention to detail — not the same thing as care — involves memory and sensitivity to nuance. The skilful combination makes everything fly.

The honing of word skills is a way of life and becomes to a writer like breathing or eating, a constant necessity and almost as automatic. I can tell I'm awake in the morning when I realize that I have already begun to polish the words and phrases drifting through my mind before my eyes are open, doing my finger exercises before I am fully conscious. As I go through the day I listen to the radio, read the newspaper, overhear people on public transit (when I'm in a city) and find myself rephrasing their expressions, taking mental notes, cherishing idiosyncrasies all the while. I may forget names (and faces) but I never forget a good line, or where I heard it. And yes, I keep a journal. Like Pigpen in "Peanuts," I am surrounded not by wisps of crud and motes of dust, but by swirling scraps of paper and shimmering shards of thought (sorry). It's part of the constant cultivation of my field.

The honing of skills requires close attention not only to words and grammar but also to the arrangements of words and thoughts in writing over the centuries as well as contemporary use. In other words, writers must read. You must continue to read voraciously, see, watch, observe what's going on around you, seek new experiences, develop a network of contacts, listen, ask questions, study, research, and make constant notes (Pigpen!). If you have access, surf the Net; drop into on-line chat groups for writers, playwrights, editors, and so on, and subscribe to their newsletters. As the years go by, you will keep on learning while you're earning. It's a never-ending story, and for all of it you must fund yourself. Rarely do expenses, if granted by a client, allow for research costs. The good news is that most of your expenses can earn you tax credits.

Experimentation is useful too. As you keep on playing with words, try different forms. I still love poetry, another sacrifice to my need for income. My first published works when I was a young stay-at-home mother were poems I "sold" (for free copies) to Canadian literary magazines, especially *Fiddlehead*. I remember one long winter in Winnipeg deliberately trying out different verse forms and rhyme schemes as finger exercises. (I wrote a sonnet about strontium 90!) Poetry helps your rhythm, which a lot of prose writers don't appreciate, but neither do poets. I once collaborated with a poet friend on an article for *Readers' Digest* and was as appalled at what he did to my sentences as he was astonished at my insistence on rhythm and balance, qualities he thought existed only in poetry.

Writing dialogue helps develop economy and a close attention to word order. You need punch lines in sentences and paragraphs as well as in people's speeches. It's important always to land on the right word. Dialogue also teaches you to distinguish between different people's voices. No two people sound the same. Neither should your characters — in novels, or plays, or even reports.

My mother used to say I was like a dog with a bone. She meant it as criticism, but it's one of my best qualities. It's a gift you can sharpen to a skill, and should, especially if you are female, this dogged determination not to be beguiled or deflected from your purpose. This is not about assertiveness training or learning to say no. This is about latching on to what you want and sticking to it. That takes skill.

CHARACTER

As a freelancer, you will be tested and you should decide in advance exactly what you will and won't do for money. It's possible you haven't fully considered the pitfalls and booby traps. Temptations will arise in seemingly innocuous ways at first, as, for example, receiving a trip with all expenses paid so that you can write a glowing travel piece about a weekend in paradise based on your glorious first-hand experience. Big newspapers, like the *New York Times*, pay their writers' expenses for assignments or buy freelance material after the fact to ensure that the enthusiasm isn't bought. Smaller papers and magazines with minuscule budgets are fair game for freebies, and I've seen their editors take the plummiest free trips for themselves. The economic facts of life being what they are, these handouts are a vital part of the magazine's budget; without them, the content would be much more limited. If you do take a paid-for assignment, make it very clear in your copy who paid for your ink, and try not to get carried away.

Plagiarism is another aspect of ethical behavior that writers must pay attention to. Not only are their souls at stake, reputations can be lost forever. I will discuss this later under copyright behaviour, because there are technical ways to cope with the problem of attribution while retaining your integrity.

How else does writing test your character? Well, of course, all writers are liars. In the best sense of the word, they lie all the time. What does that mean, "in the best sense of the word"? It means tell stories, make-believe, pretend, exaggerate, project, cause a suspension of disbelief in order to create all the delightful fantasies conjured up with a single, simple phrase: *what if*. But there are boundaries to the storytelling and we cross them at our peril.

Perhaps it's easier to see the boundaries of fiction. Readers more willingly put themselves into the hands — eyes, ears — of an acknowledged storyteller. This isn't real, this incense of illusion swirling around us and rising with our dreams as we sit around the fire listening to the words of the storyteller. It's just a story. We can relax, let go, and trust the narrator. Until proven otherwise, all narrators are trustworthy.

In fiction, what the writer has to be careful of is not to tell it too close to life. A roman à clef may be fun to solve, as we identify well-known, real-life persons in the characters described. But if a writer is too accurate or vicious, there's trouble, in the form of a libel suit, some-times even if — maybe even especially if — the material is funny. Most people don't like to be laughed at, particularly in print.

For characters in a story, it helps if you avoid real names, that is, the names of real people. How do you manage that? There isn't a sound you can make with your mouth that isn't a word in some language. Similarly, there are so many people in the world now that surely any name you make up exists somewhere. Look at Grace Metallious. She made up a name for a character in her book *Peyton Place* and met a man with that name when she had almost finished writing the novel. She told him about her made-up character and they both laughed about it. But when one of the most delicious trash novels of the century hit the best-seller list, the man sued her for the use of his name. In subsequent editions Metallious used a different one.

Here is my solution to this problem. For surnames I use map names, not physical features like Hard Rock or Clear Lake, but people-sounding names (Trossachs, Craighurst, Schönberg). Most places, after all, were named after the people who discovered or founded them. You can estab-lish any ethnic identity you need this way. If anyone tries to sue you, point to a map. I know another writer who says she uses the telephone book, choosing names at random. I don't think that method is as safe.

As for first names, I do like symbolic ones for lead characters. Few people get the point but *I* know and it gives me a valid reason when questioned. A director wanted to change the name of the protagonist in my one-man play about a mentally challenged young man because the actor playing it was from Lebanon and had a slight accent and the direc-tor thought a Lebanese name might excuse it. When I explained that I chose Jason after the hero in Greek mythology who was searching for the Golden Fleece, since my character was in search of something equally difficult, the director backed down immediately, looking, I might add, pleased. Directors and editors are suckers for symbols.

Even when you use ordinary people, as opposed to genuine celebrities, you're still not safe from lawsuits. If you put your Aunt Shirley into a book, she might be upset if you make her too fat or find fault with her cooking and she might cut you out of her will, or worse. Most fiction writers settle for composites of people they know and will tell you how characters suffer a sea change once they take over the story.

I dwell on nomenclature and its concomitant problems in the discussion of character because you, the writer, must be sure you are not being merely vindictive or getting even. You have been given a powerful instrument; don't use it as a cruel weapon just because you think you're safe hiding behind the curtain of a story. There's a human being on the other side of the arras.

Somehow we expect plodding truth from the non-fiction writer, but several heinous cases have revealed the lies of journalists. *The Great Solar Scam* drew attention to the "facts" written by science reporter Julian Cribb for *The Australian* in which he promoted solar energy with unfounded and misleading claims. *The Sunday Herald Sun*'s writer Veronica Matheson whitewashed Dr. Helen Caldicott, her antinuclear stance and her pro-Soviet activities. So many lies have been published about the disaster at Chernobyl and the Gulf War that it is impossible to sift out the truth about those events. It would be untrue to call the untruths mere exaggeration. The question has arisen as to how far exaggerating, rearranging, condensing, or omitting facts can be taken before the content becomes totally dishonest. And what about Israel and Palestine? Will we learn the truth? Not, it seems, from journalists.

For some non-fiction work, the question never arises, but the boundaries and limits are becoming broader and less clear. For reports, manuals, corporate writing, and straight reportage, it's simple: just the facts, please. But when we get to personal columns, the so-called "familiar" essay, and "think" pieces about current social problems with anecdotes and illustrations "from life," the lines blur and non-fiction becomes creative. In fact, creative non-fiction is considered a separate genre now. Is it fictionalized fact or is it fiction based on real events? Probably both or either, but you have to be careful. I'm still talking character — yours.

I think composites are death in non-fiction, an insidious kind of lie that some editors encourage. For instance, a favourite method of illustrating problems in magazine articles is to present an assortment of examples from life identified by their full, real names if the interviewees allow it, by made-up names with some kind of individual disclaimer: "not her real name," or "we'll call him Sue," or a general note, "because of extremely tender testimony, the names of all the people involved in this case have been changed to protect their families." Sometimes a sample person is referred to as D. or Mrs. P., some appropriate initial usually meaningful to the writer. These are supposed to be real people, real stories. Once you move into initials, though, you will be tempted to use composites — or perhaps not you, but your editor.

A few years ago I was invited by a women's magazine to write a piece about widowhood because I was by that time Canada's best-known widow. When she gave me the assignment, the non-fiction editor told me she wanted two recent wrenching examples of bleeding widowhood to use as horror stories, preferably with financial problems (not hard to find), one old, one young. I usually have on tap any number of fresh widows so I started phoning and looking around and found two women who were willing to be interviewed but not named. I wrote the piece and sent it in. It came back to me with a more specific shopping list: my editor wanted an older woman whose husband had died of a long, lingering illness and whose insurance had thus been used up; and a younger woman whose husband had died suddenly before he had made adequate provisions for his wife. I said I didn't have any of those in stock but I had a number of women I could draw from my fan mail whose cases and problems I could describe anonymously.

I rewrote the piece, drawing from several women for examples of some of the things that can happen and going on from there with my cautionary words of wisdom. The piece came back again, rewritten, turning the disparate examples into two or three composite (read: false) cases and also turning my honest advice into Band-Aid solutions. My statement has always been that after the death of a loved one, life will never be the same. My editor thought that was too bleak. Do this, do this, do this, and do that, the article now said, and you'll be fine. Next case. I said that the article was now a lie and asked to have my byline removed. The piece never ran.

The magazine sent me my full fee, not a kill fee,[1] and the editor dropped me a note saying she was sorry that her idea of a service piece and mine didn't jibe. To my mind, that was not service, that was disservice. Bland, blind comfort is useless. Fudges are lies. Composites are unethical. So is taking words out of a writer's mouth — or putting them in.

On another, earlier occasion when too many words had been put in my mouth and the slant of the piece totally changed from what another editor and I had agreed it would be, I also asked for removal of my name or of the article. In that case, it was printed under a pseudonym.

Yet another general magazine tried to put words in before I'd even written them. Shortly after I had arrived in Toronto in 1975, eager and hungry, I got a go-ahead on a piece I wanted to write about the first-ever International Women's Year (so designated by the United Nations) just rounding the corner to the finish line. There was plenty of time; the magazine was still a general monthly. I had scarcely begun my research when an editor called, asked me how I was doing, and then told me to come up with a negative assessment. I said I couldn't guarantee that because I hadn't learned enough yet. He said either come up with a put-down or don't bother writing it. I said I wouldn't bother writing it. There are times when saying no is more important than money.

These are case histories to do with assigned pieces when an editor tried to wield my pen. What about the temptations of the marketplace where you, the writer, are tempted to make your story better than it is in order to sell it? You don't have all the information you need to make a convincing

---

1   Half the agreed-upon amount if an assigned article doesn't meet the editor's expectations.

case; it would be so easy to fill in the gaps by making something up. Or you don't have good victims; why not invent some and say you've changed all the names to protect them? A Pulitzer Prize-winner of a few years back was stripped of her prize for doing just that. Don't let mere fear of discovery be your only deterrent, although you should know by now you will always get caught. Sooner or later someone will find you out. Even if you think you could get away with it, don't try. You wouldn't, I'm sure.

> [from] THE WRITER'S PRAYER:
> Give me the courage to write clean and true, regardless of what all others around me are writing. Help me to remember always that words have the power to destroy — or build; the power to spread ignorance — or dispense knowledge; the power to darken the world with hate — or light it with love.[2]

What about ghostwriting, where you put your words in another person's mouth for money? I did ghostwrite one book but found the experience degrading, especially after the person's agent cut in half my skimpy $2,000 fee because, after all, it was the person's life and work and all I had to do was put them down on paper (and my agent agreed!). As it was, the only way I was able to write the book was to pretend that the person was a character in one of my plays. The moral to that story is that versatile as I have to be as a freelancer, some jobs simply do not suit me. You'll probably make a similar discovery, that there are some things you would rather not do. You will have to consider each genre, subject, and form as you come to it.

I'm just giving you a few warnings of things that can happen.

Like the time another editor, a friendly man, wanted me to do a number on the Imperial Order, Daughters of the Empire (IODE) for a now-defunct weekend magazine. The editor had grown up in Guelph thinking that all the ladies of the IODE were really funny, with big navels

---

2 Copyright 1972 by Writer's Digest School, pinned to my bulletin board ever since.

from supporting flags, and holier-than-thou expressions from being such exclusive members of an obsolete club. I did my research and found a vital organization doing good work in the community. They were post-war but not all postmenopausal, with a good mix of young and mature members, and I said so in my article. My editor sent it back for a rewrite demanding something funnier. I wrote a funnier piece but still admiring, unwilling to deny my grandmother, who was a founding member of her chapter in Manitoba. Still no sale. So then I wrote a really funny piece about the editor and his perception of the IODE. I received a kill fee.

Two offers gave me less pause — the ten minutes it took a book publisher to make a pitch. At a party somewhere (she does her best work at parties), she offered me a fast $25,000 to ghostwrite Margaret Trudeau's second autobiography. When I heard the ground rules, which I can't go into because they would be libellous, I refused, much as I could have used the money. A few years later the same publisher offered me a similar quick-bucks assignment ghosting Cathy Smith's story, describing the fatal dose that killed John Belushi. I didn't like the subject matter or the journalistic attitude that panders to people's prurient voyeurism. I don't score on sleaze.

I'm giving you all these little vignettes, insights, and anecdotes to show you what I encountered, all unsuspecting, and what I learned, too slowly, about aspects of the writing life that most writing books don't tell you. Knowing what to expect may enable you to make quicker, clearer decisions, informed in advance by your knowledge of yourself and your own limitations and beliefs. You have a core of integrity, perhaps untapped, untested. You may have a vague (unwritten?) code of ethics, certain standards you will not break, certain bounds beyond which you would refuse to venture. Sometimes, though, as a new writer — that is, a writer just starting out and eager to please — you find you have to establish limits. Otherwise, events can get ahead of you, things can go slowly awry, little slips become slovenly errors, and small winks become blind acceptance. Embroidery, embellishment, and exaggeration may lead too easily to twisted takes, skewed slants, and deliberate deception. Small compromises and gentle assaults can chip away at a writer's character; small victories and gentle resistance will strengthen you. Be careful.

The trick, of course, is to maintain your standards and be true to yourself. Try to maintain a through-line, some sense of continuity in what you're doing, never losing sight of your prime target, whatever it may be. If you deviate too far from your chosen field, you may feel you are slumming and your frame of mind will have an effect on your writing. Give your work and your audience the respect they deserve. You begin with aesthetics, trying to write as well as you can. You invariably end with ethics, being true to standards like honesty and integrity, stuff like that.

Don't forget that if you expect your readers to pay for your words and to trust you, you must never lose your respect for them — the readers or the words. The creator of Archie and Mehitabel, poet/columnist Don Marquis, said that if you want to get rich from writing you should write the sort of thing that's read by persons who move their lips when they're reading to themselves. Amusing, but too cynical and not true. "Serious" writers tend to trash romances and thrillers, although most readers and critics respect mysteries. One thing is certain: If you don't believe in what you're writing, you won't be able to write it, not convincingly. As a writer-in-library a few times, I've read and critiqued several attempts at romance writing by earnest amateurs. While they had other faults, they maintained tone and belief in a way a nonbeliever cannot. If you are a nonbeliever and sell out by selling yourself, no one's going to respect you in the morning.

There's a clause in cookbook contracts whereby you promise not to poison anyone with your bizarre use of food; no one ever makes you sign that about the careless wielding of your ideas, but it should probably be in every agreement. You can keep a covenant with yourself by refusing to damage your integrity by going along with any sleaze that's offered you in the name of making a living.

Isaac Bashevis Singer, the great Yiddish storyteller, is supposed to have had a standard by which he wrote, a touchstone, if you like: "Will little children die from it?" If he thought they would be harmed by what he wrote, he didn't write it. Define harm.

You must ask yourself: Will you write pornography, abuse, misogyny, graphic sex or violence? What about gratuitous misogynist violence? I'm not trying to muzzle you, I'm just asking, but not lightly. You don't have to put your head in the ink pot and pretend the dark side doesn't exist; you do have to decide how you're going to deal with the darkness. You may not smoke or drink or do drugs, but it's possible you will write about individuals who do, and make them human. Vegetarian yourself, you're not afraid to deal with a carnivorous character who is not a bloodthirsty monster. Perhaps you're a small-l liberal, but will that prevent you from writing a positive representation of a right-wing Christian fundamentalist?

I am not recommending self-censorship if the result is to cripple your imagination or hamper your freedom. I would suggest, however, that you (re-)read Milton's essay "Areopagitica" (1644) on the liberty of unlicensed printing. "I cannot praise," he wrote, "a fugitive and cloistered virtue unexercised and unbreathed." By all means, show us evil, that we may know good, and "Give me the liberty to know, to utter, and to argue freely according to conscience, above all liberties."

But bear in mind also what he wrote in a later essay:

> None can love freedom heartily, but good men [persons];
> the rest love not freedom, but license.

Your view of life will influence your choice of subject and how you write about it. (The French novelist Colette once commented that we do not choose our subjects; our subjects choose us.) Most laypeople, i.e., non-writers, can get along comfortably for years without seriously confronting their beliefs or behaviour. Writers, however, have to face a truth of some kind every day: justice, fairness, honesty, and other human values come up much more often. Well, maybe they don't come up any more often, but they can't be fudged, not when you're writing about them.

At the end of my play *Time Bomb*, about some ex-mental patients in a boardinghouse, my heroine defends herself from a man who is trying to kill her with the broken end of a beer bottle. He is stoned and drunk, not very well coordinated, but powerful. She is hyper, alert, and terrified. The two combatants dance and feint, climbing up and over beds, stumbling over obstacles, until the man falls, crashing onto his back and losing his weapon. The young woman grabs the bottle and kneels over him, arm raised, ready to smash it into his face. He urges her to go ahead and kill him.

She holds her position, arm raised and shaking, her whole body caught in the balance for a long moment ...

"If I kill you, I kill myself," she says, and lowers her arm.

I have seen play endings where the blood is running on the stage, ambulances and retribution are on the way, and death prevails. I choose to opt for life. In an era when violent death sells books, television, and movies, I have been accused of soft sentimentality. I personally think it is far harder for someone in a situation like that, blood and adrenaline pumping, to turn away from violence. That takes not less courage, but more. It might even cause a viewer to question current values — or fashionable clichés. As moral writer John Gardner wrote: "If we are unable to distinguish between true morality — life-affirming, just, and compassionate behavior — and trivial moral fashion, we begin to doubt morality itself."[3]

Even Tolstoy wrote that art should cause violence to be set aside. (I say *even* because he didn't treat his wife very well.) I'm not saying you can't write about violence, but you don't have to worship it. I'm not violent enough. I tend, in my first drafts (of plays) to shy away from confrontation. I always have to write in more conflict. I have to screw my characters' courage to the sticking point, as Shakespeare said, and make them fight for what they want.

What do you want? Remember that you are not only selling a product, you are a product in yourself; you're putting a piece of yourself into everything you create. That self — the creator — had better have staying power, also some idea of basic morality.

---

3   From the essay "Moral Fiction," which appeared in *The Saturday Review of Books* in 1978, adapted from Gardner's book *On Moral Fiction*.

Doomsayers claim we are living in an increasingly godless society; John Gardner says *un-goded*. Perhaps it's a no-name god, generic, suitable for all sizes and sects. If we don't have some sense of a few eternal verities, we're going to become unanchored weather vanes, flying off in the first stiff wind and finding it difficult to nail our truth to the mast. I may not like violence but I can withstand it and I can hold to what I believe and write what I believe. You don't have to share any of my beliefs, but you must be aware that your belief, or lack of it, is part of your character and will affect your writing. Find your sticking point. This has everything to do with surviving as a writer. You have to like the person who survives.

DISCIPLINE

One of the questions I am most frequently asked, both by beginning writers and by writers who are just setting out on their own, is where do I find the discipline to write every day. Right off, get rid of the idea that writing is some sort of casual activity you dally in when the mood or inspiration strikes you. Few laypeople see your work as a routine job with regular, long hours. No one realizes how hard it is to write when you don't feel like it — about as hard as getting up and going to work when you don't feel like it.

> WRITING IS MERE JOTTING
> "You just jot down ideas as they occur to you. The jotting
> is simplicity itself — it is the occurring which is difficult."
> — STEPHEN LEACOCK

What's harder is making the time work. When you have an assignment, it's slightly easier because you do have a deadline. You can't goof off for too long. No copy, no cheque. Even so, the temptation is to keep on doing research, or to find one more good angle from someone, somewhere, or to change the typewriter ribbon (if you can even find one these days!) or the printer cartridge, or to sharpen all the pencils, as Ernest Hemingway is supposed to have done, or to hell with it, go and have coffee or lunch with someone and start tomorrow.

There's always peripheral work to do that you can use to justify, or at least rationalize, your reluctance to put pen to paper or fingers to keyboard. It can keep you so busy, especially between assignments, that you never notice you're not actually writing.

A SMALL PARABLE
Once upon a time there was a man, a successful writer, who counted the number of hours he actually spent writing each day. It came to 45 minutes, so he killed himself.

Such apocryphal humour is based on truth. The truth is that you are performing a slow gavotte with your writing machine: advance and retreat, advance and retreat, and sometimes it resembles a dance of death. You wonder who's going to give in first.

You have two responsibilities as a writer: one, meeting others' expectations, and two, meeting your own. Both require discipline. The latter duty is much more difficult, especially once you go to work for yourself. As a writer you can justify almost any activity for the sake of Art. You have clearly outlined work to do, also a clearly defined need and no time to dally, and yet ...

There are times when your chosen life allows you to idle over a second cup of coffee and watch the passing parade; goof off to a movie in the middle of the day; drive or walk around aimlessly looking at houses or scenery; read a trashy novel; get drunk or high or stoned; have an affair — and do it all in the respectable name of life experience. But it's called procrastinating, not only putting things off and wasting time but developing deferral to an art form.

There's a line I read somewhere that I think must have been written for writers, something about having "a tool too keen for timid safety."

You can repeat that like a mantra if you need to rationalize your bad habits. It doesn't accomplish your purpose but it allows you to indulge your bad habits with a clearer conscience. But not for too long.

The trouble, as you will discover, is that the person you work for is an unforgiving taskmaster. You get less time off than you ever did in a nine-to-five job, and when you steal some to go to your grandmother's funeral, there's no fooling the nitpicker. Even so, even with that overactive conscience hovering over your shoulder, you'll find that constant self-discipline is tricky. When you become a freelancer you have nothing but spare time and it's heady. You have to learn how to spend it wisely.

The Accidental Shepherd

I knew someone, a would-be playwright, who inherited a place by the sea in Nova Scotia and decided he would take a year off to go and write a Canadian masterpiece. He spent a busy year trimming the hedges and feeding the sheep, of which he had one. The next year he sold his retreat and went back to work.

There's a fine line between self-discipline and workaholism, and I'm not sure it can be clearly drawn for anyone who works freelance. Depends what you're doing and how you feel about it. It also depends on whether you live alone or with your family, who won't let you entirely disappear. Just because you love what you're doing doesn't mean it isn't work. You still get tired and need your sleep, especially when it doesn't feel like work, when it's going well and you are totally immersed and enjoying it, oblivious of time. It only feels like overwork, that is, pressure, when you're short of time, with too tight a deadline or too many things piled up all demanding immediate attention, or when you break a promise to a mate or child, or when an employer/client who had been on the back burner for months suddenly crooks a finger, hands you an assignment and wants it yesterday. That doesn't require self-discipline; that requires self-abnegation, also juggling.

Discipline is doing what you say you're going to do, when you say you're going to do it, and delivering the goods as promised. We'll talk about realistic assessments of work, and the time required to do it, later. I'm superstitious about deadlines; I've never missed one in my life and I have this terrible fear that if I ever do I'll never write again. Mind you, I was recently late by two days on a copy-edit return (more flexible than an actual manuscript deadline) because I had a root canal and lost four workdays. But I had met the original deadline for the first draft of that book in spite of being stranded away from home overnight and half a day while the gas tank on my car was replaced. Things happen.

When they do, you must keep your clients informed. If you absolutely cannot come up with a complete, finished product as promised, then give them something on account. Give them what is done and be sure it's so good that they'll be a) thrilled, and b) eager for the next installment. Obviously, we're talking assignments here, meeting your obligations. It's harder to be disciplined when you have only yourself to report to.

Into every freelance writer's life lean times must fall. In fact, of course, it never ceases to be feast or famine. Either you're so busy you can't lift your head above the sea of paper you're going to drown in, or you are slogging across a desert with no oasis in sight. That's harder. You have to fill the mails with queries and product, seeking your next source of income; you have to keep working, creating something new, preferably something you've been eager to get at and needed free time for; you have to keep up your hopes as well as your courage while you spend enormous amounts of money you don't have on postage, faxes, and couriers, sending out material and ideas for sale, accompanied by bright, eager messages asking (begging!) for an assignment. And then you're afraid to say no.

This is an occupational hazard of any self-employed person. Actors and office temps and freelance editors and anyone else who works at other people's beck and call find it hard to refuse a beck when it's offered. The first time you say no, in fact, is going to be a milestone because it means you trust yourself and have lost your initial fear. Fear is harder to live with than overwork. Work stops when you complete it. Fear won't go away without a different kind of effort.

Fear is all in your head, you know, and there's no room in your head for it because you have to muster every synapse you can to take care of all the information you need to be an effective writer. Storage and retrieval are physical problems and I will discuss how to deal with your files and research. Using your head requires more than a good filing system, and I'll get to that next. First, however, as part of your *stuff*, your preparation for the writing life, you must consider your education.

EDUCATION

Okay, here's a corny answer to a thorny question. When I started university, the dean of Arts and Science addressed the first-year student body at some sort of welcoming ceremony by analyzing what an education will do for you:

- It will teach you to entertain yourself.
- It will teach you to entertain others.
- It will teach you to entertain ideas.

The good news is that you don't need a university education to acquire these abilities, nor does everyone who has a degree automatically achieve them. The term for a self-taught person is autodidact. There have been some awesome examples both in previous centuries and the present one — the Brontës, Benjamin Franklin, Alden Nowlan, Mary Wollstonecraft — but they are rare and they are flawed, and also quite often belligerent.

Would-be writers often ask if they really need a post-secondary education; the answer is maybe not, but the years spent at university do give you time to hone a few skills and take a few gratuitous risks without damaging your career. The training period is not marking time; call it an apprenticeship. Apart from knowledge, which you can, admittedly, pick up at random by yourself, a formal education will also give you an inkling of the discipline you need to be a freelancer.

When I first began to attempt to live by my words, a feeling I remember from university days came back to me: the pressure of that little black cloud of piled-up work nagging at me to be done, following me where I went, like the rainstorm that follows Joe Btfsplk in the comic strip, "Li'l Abner." I could lift it temporarily by escaping into a novel or a movie, but it was there waiting for me and back overhead within two steps out of the theatre. I had almost forgotten it until I faced my first book deadline, and there it was. Suddenly I was back in university again and time was my enemy, or friend, depending on how disciplined I was. Fortunately, I had learned that lesson well.

Another lesson a formal education teaches you is the method for doing effective research. As a writer, whether of fiction or non-, you will need this skill. You will find yourself less panicked by what you don't know and more capable of searching for what you need. While you're still at school, you will have time to learn to use the available resources of other people, libraries, newspapers, and computers. (God bless search engines and links!) You will become adept at spreading your fingers and nets to find more. Not that anyone can't learn how to do this, but it will save you time, and later, angst, if you've given yourself the time to learn it well. In school, you're free to poke around, explore, browse, investigate, play, and ask a lot of questions. You may never have such wide-ranging freedom for learning opportunities again.

You also are encouraged to think, but not merely formally. You learn the give-and-take process of thinking on your feet (or seat) in seminars, workshops, coffee bars, and pubs, exchanging ideas, trying out theories, arguing, and defending your beliefs. Being told you're full of shit won't cost you anything and can be very exhilarating. You learn that what you've learned to value does not necessarily jibe with what your respected cohorts believe. You learn, therefore, to cherish differences and to be humble in the face of others' convictions while hanging on to your own, but being open to change. Autodidacts seldom learn these skills, and they're what keep you humble.

That's the real secret of an education — humility. You need it to save you from yourself as you begin to fly on your own. Remember Mark Twain's comment about how much his old man learned as the boy grew up? An education works like that with a reverse application, and you can feel it happening to you. In first and second year, you know everything; by the time you graduate, you have learned how much you don't know. The rest of your life will be spent trying to learn enough. Use your head.

PART THREE

Using Your Head

*In Which the Writer Tells
How to Oil the Machine*

You may have all the education in the world but if you can't tap it, where are you? You also may consider yourself very disciplined; that is, you are capable of sitting alone for hours and hours doing something with words. Head and hand, eyes and heart, how do you get them connected? Is there a phone number you can use to dial up your friendly neighborhood Muse and get her to come over and give you a kick-start? Or maybe she comes, but at random moments, never there when you need her, certainly not on command, or even request. Okay, let's start by ...

USING THE SUBCONSCIOUS

Does this happen to you? Someone calls you when you're writing, and when you answer the phone, asks, "Were you asleep?" No, you were writing, but you sound as if you're at the bottom of a well. That's because you were probably deep in alpha waves, a good place to surf when you're being creative. You tell your friend to hang up and you dive in again.

TM, or transcendental meditation, invaded North American minds in the mid to late seventies, just as I was trying to make emotional and economic sense of my life. Westerners trying to latch onto Eastern modes thought a mantra was a magic carpet to peace of mind and everybody had a favourite guru. I actually came at it by accident, like everything else I did. Seeking some comfort for my grief after the death of my husband, I had attended a weekend of spiritual healing at a Christian Education Centre in southwestern Ontario where the best thing that happened was my purchase of a small book of meditations. They were not TM, not Eastern in their approach, but rather rooted in Western theology, in the work of Christian mystics like Saint John of the Cross (*The Cloud of Unknowing*) and Saint Teresa of Avila. Realizing the nature of the discipline, I bought a lay book, Robert Orenstein's *The Psychology of Consciousness*, and a couple of spiritual books, and taught myself to meditate. That pursuit of emotional solace was followed by a writing discovery, that the well of the subconscious could be deliberately tapped.

The creative writing teacher Dorothea Brande (1893–1948) published her book *Becoming a Writer* in 1934. Reissued in 1981 with a foreword by John Gardner, it has been in print ever since, and that's good for several reasons, but for me especially because of Brande's use of the subconscious.[4] Ahead of her time with this idea and fifty years before anyone started deliberately dabbling with brain waves, Brande recommended harnessing them. "To begin with," she writes, "you must teach the unconscious to flow into the channel of writing." This is where alpha waves come in.

The German psychiatrist Hans Berger first demonstrated the electrical activity of the brain in 1929, five years before Brande published her book, but she didn't mention him, nor did his peers pay much attention to his discovery of the brain rhythms he called alpha waves. Since then other scientists have isolated and identified at least three other brain-wave patterns.

> *Alpha waves* are background activity, most visible (with the aid of an electroencephalograph) during dream-sleep or relaxation with the eyes closed.

> *Delta waves* are slow-moving and regular, characteristic of the deepest levels of sleep.

> *Theta waves* are most commonly apparent in children to the age of puberty, with a velocity somewhere between alpha and delta. Theta waves in an adult may signal brain damage or an immature personality (or a writer?).

> *Beta waves* are small, fast patterns, indicating stress. Most of us walk around in beta.

---

4   Brande used the word *unconscious*, but we would say *subconscious*: "existing in the mind and affecting thoughts, attitudes, or behavior not consciously felt" (Gage). The unconscious has been taken over by Freud, Jung, et al.

It has been discovered that Eastern (but not only Eastern) practices of meditation can increase alpha and theta waves, resulting in lessened anxiety, which is what most people seek, but also in clearer access to the subconscious. This is where writers mine for gold.

I had been using this meditation technique for years without fully understanding what I was doing; you may have been doing the same. It began when I was writing exams at university. I finished my studying at night, managed to get a little sleep, woke up and wrote an exam. My subconscious had been given time to sort things out and then, on cue, delivered what I needed. That was my first introduction to alpha waves but I didn't know it then. I began to do it automatically when I was writing; I would finish my research, go over all the material, often setting myself an assignment, like a good lead, sleep on it, and start to write the next day, lead in hand. Sometimes, however, I couldn't afford to wait those extra hours, sometimes I was through my research and preparation and it was only the middle of the day, or not even noon. What to do?

Meditation worked just as well. I found that wiping the mind cleared it of obstacles and debris and gave my subconscious time to deal with the material. When I was ready to write an article, I would lie down on the floor, cross my hands across my breast like the Lily Maid of Astolat, and meditate for fifteen to twenty minutes. Then I would get up and write. It's a good trick and I recommend it.

Dorothea Brande also offers a way to start your day. Her advice is really a method of catching the subconscious unawares. She writes:

> The best way to do this is to rise half an hour, or a full hour, earlier than you customarily rise. Just as soon as you can — and without talking, without reading the morning's paper, without picking up the book you laid aside the night before — begin to write.

Her purpose is to find out what's going on in there. It's a good way to mine ideas. Ideally, you'll make a new discovery; get it while it's hot, catch it before it's cool. But it's also useful to kick-start your writing day with a work in progress, getting in the mode early and keeping on with it. Perhaps you can't keep on if you still have a day job to go to. But if you start your day with writing, whatever you're working on will stay with you and you will not fall out of the mode. If you're at home, the same approach applies with even better results, that is, with more applied time. You can write for a couple of hours before you break for breakfast or chores. Of course, some writers prefer to write at night. That's okay. Most people tend to slip into alpha waves after midnight whether they're actually in bed asleep or not. If that's your favourite time to write, just reset your engagement calendar and make your appointment with creation for after eleven.

Another way to ensure that you start first thing in the morning is to visualize doing it the night before. See yourself getting up in the morning and sitting down to write. Give yourself an assignment: the next chapter, a new article, an idea to play around with. Choose something, but do not choose to rewrite or research. That's a terrible waste of good alpha waves! Save your rewrites for later in the day when your editorial mode kicks in; research is for evening so you sleep on it and sort it out. You want to catch your most creative self without all the tramlines and buzzes of your everyday beta waves. Write first. Don't think, don't putter, don't do anything else. Just do it.

GENERATING IDEAS

Another question I am often asked can be answered in part from the same source. Where do I find my ideas? This deserves a larger discussion, but I can say that Dorothea Brande helps. When I'm wondering what to do next, or when I want to find out what's going on down there in my subconscious, I make an appointment with myself for a "free-fall." That is, I get up earlier and I sit down to write, as usual, but without a plan. I wait and see what comes up.

Free-fall is the term Canadian writer W.O. Mitchell gave to this kind of surfing on your alpha waves: freewheeling, flying, scavenging. You will probably find, as I have, that your next work is lying there under the surface, ready to be dredged up. *Dredge* is a good word. When I go to write the first draft of a new play, I compare it to dredging up my bone marrow. I've never had my bone marrow dredged, but the procedure has been described to me, and I think the image is apt.

Before that happens, however, I have put a lot of time into thinking. Some of this is best described as cluster thinking: how to take a concept and turn it into an idea, take an idea and shape it into a project, take a project and develop it into a finished work. Whole books have been written about cluster thinking, tapping the right side of the brain, giving a kick-start to your thinker. I'll tell you how I do it. Start small.

Begin with a blank piece of paper (better than a computer screen). Write a key word in the middle of the page. Then start brainstorming around it, using word association, synonyms, phrases, lateral thinking, anything that occurs to you. Now, on a fresh sheet of paper, write down some of these associative words. Then, using your favourite thesaurus (Roget's is mine, for this purpose), look up all the words, write down all the synonyms and look up each one, noting the nuances. Back in my essay-writing days I used to look up the main words in an assignment in just this way. Often I found in the various synonyms the clues to the outline and the argument.

On yet more paper, take some of the words and synonyms you like and cluster around them. The cluster is a bouquet of related ideas clustered around the central word or words. Include random thoughts, your best lateral thinking; refer to clippings you have been collecting; find apt quotations; look over your seed beds — your germinating collection of ideas, images, and mental tchotchkes you had to save. I own several dictionaries of quotations, which are arranged not according to the people who said them but by subjects. One is even called a thesaurus of quotations. Sometimes — often — these sayings will trigger a thought or illuminate an aspect of the idea I hadn't thought of.

If you're writing an article, your initial work is almost done; you know what it's really about — the slant. Next you have to organize the topic by the main points, according to those key words, do the relevant research and fill in the blanks; in other words, write an intelligent, reasoned, informative, and/or entertaining article!

This may sound like a lot of work, but once you know what you're doing, it's half done. Very little of your research will be wasted because you know exactly what you're looking for. Of course, in the case of a play or novel, you've only just begun. By this time you probably have a good idea of whom or what you're dealing with, usually whom, because you can't write a dramatic piece about an abstract idea. (It doesn't sell.) So now, check these words and sayings and your own scribbled reactions against the characters in your head. Soon you start hearing their voices, expressing ideas you wish you had thought of! I'll stop here, because this is cluster thinking, not Playwriting 101. You're on your own as far as the writing is concerned.

WRITER'S BLOCK

How do your get around Writer's Block? Another common question. You might also ask what the difference is between Writer's Block and lack of discipline. A lot, sometimes.

A True Confession

When my play *Mark* was accepted, I realized one scene was missing that I had to write before rehearsals began, a confrontation between the mother and the daughter. I hit the worst block of my life as I resisted emotions I had to deal with concerning my relationship with my own mother. I didn't go near the typewriter for two weeks. The block finally broke, not on command, certainly not conveniently. One minute I was having lunch with my family, the next I was at the typewriter with the words pouring out of me and the tears streaming down my face. The scene wrote itself and I didn't change a word, not even when the actors in rehearsal balked and suggested changes. They and the director argued while I listened, and then they put it back together, exactly as written.

Actually, there are two kinds of Writer's Block: one you can find ways to detour, using tricks to keep yourself working; the other, like my emotional one, you can't.

Back when I was a housewife I used to think I never suffered from Writer's Block. I just never called it "block," that's all. I called it polishing the silver or baking brownies or making Halloween costumes, which goes to show you how desperate I was, because I can't sew. Once I even polished all the doors in the house — *plywood* doors.

So how do you get around or over a block? Around is better. One of the sayings of Alcoholics Anonymous, I am told, is this: "Move a muscle and the mind will follow," meaning, I suppose, that the best way to do something is to begin doing it. This applies to writing.

> Jabbering away on paper, one gets tricked into feeling interested, all at once in something one is saying and behold, the magic waters are flowing again.
> — JOHN GARDNER, *Becoming a Novelist*

I do peripheral things, a little more research, but also — better, more useful — more cluster thinking. Maybe I rewrite my outline. I start scribbling — anything! I use pen and paper usually to do this but you can type if you feel like it. Just start writing. You can start by writing "I can't think of anything to say," and go on from there. You can write "Now is the time for all good men to come to the aid of the party," or that sentence so dear to typists' hearts: "The quick brown fox jumped over the lazy dogs." I heard of one writer who always wrote SHIT at the top of his page every morning. Then he was so ashamed of himself that he wrote hard to make up for that useless word. Now he'd just hit the delete button. Of course, if you're *wired*, that is, on the Internet, you can always look up another useful fact or fancy. Just be careful you don't end up forever surfing; that's not very creative. Research like this is, after all, avoidance behaviour. I recommend turning to your journal first.

What if that doesn't work?

Do a crossword puzzle. The late Canadian novelist and Governor General's Award winner Marion Engel used to do jigsaw puzzles. The American academic Carl van Doren thought that walking on a beach and picking up shells or pebbles was an ideal thing to do when (not) writing. Some people like to make love; others find it a drain. A nice, mindless activity takes the pressure off. Don't worry; even when you're not writing, you're still writing. But as you know, danger lurks here because you get better at it — not writing. My line is that it takes much longer not to write a play than to write one. Once all my messing about is done (dancing the gavotte), it takes me from three to five days (I'm talking twelve-hour days) to write the first draft of a new play, and two weeks to a month to write a non-fiction book. This is not rewriting; this is breaking the sound barrier. I think it takes as much energy to break into a new project as it does to launch a rocket, figuratively speaking, of course.

Are we talking block or are we talking incubating?

> As for my next book, I am going to hold myself from writing it till I have it impending in me: grown heavy in my mind like a ripe pear; pendant, gravid, asking to be cut or it will fall.
> — VIRGINIA WOOLF, *A Writer's Diary*

That's incubation and there's nothing wrong with it. Of course, it can't be done without a day job or a supportive spouse. On your own you can't afford to wait too long. Instead, treat yourself like a prisoner. Create your own retreat. Cancel all engagements, turn on the voice mail, be a recluse. There is no escape for you, except through the magic tunnel of your mind.

This is where Brande and your meditation techniques will help you through, with perhaps a little lateral thinking on the side. I've often used Edward de Bono's idea of sidestepping the issue I need to confront. Think of yourself as creating a parallel universe and then slide into the one you really want to deal with.

You just have to stay with it. The harsh fact is, as you will see, that no self-respecting writer can claim to be a writer who doesn't write a minimum of four hours a day. Stick that in your floppy disk.

I know, I know, sometimes you just can't. Like when you're doing your accounts or income tax, or flying around on a promotion tour, or digging up information, or writing letters and queries. The actual business of writing is in another chapter, but the daunting fact is to be faced here, that some days you simply don't have time to write, actually write. Again, that's why retreats are good, or an approximation thereof, because they involve a withdrawal of your creative self from the hurly-burly of everyday living. Far from the madding crowd you can concentrate for hours and hours on pure writing. So when I say write four hours a day every day, that may at times translate to eight to twelve hours daily for a solid week and then a complete change of pace to a marketing mode or an accounting frenzy. Allow for that and be good to yourself. Just remember, always, that you are in business. The hours spent in beta are what make all the alpha rollers possible.

PART FOUR

The Writing Life

*In Which, Back to the Wall, the Writer
Faces Forward, the Future and Fate*

PARABLE

Once upon a time there was a poor baker and his wife who were having trouble making a living. One sad day the baker told his wife that they'd reached the end of their bin.

"Tomorrow will be our last day," he said. "We have no money for supplies."

A beggar came along asking for shelter, and though the baker and his wife had little to spare they took him in and shared what they had with him.

In the morning, the beggar thanked the couple, saying before he left, "Whatever you do first, that you will do all day."

There wasn't enough flour to bake bread. The baker decided they would make a few cookies for a sick little girl down the street. Passersby were lured into the shop by the fragrant aroma of the cookies. The baker and his wife were too busy to serve them, so the customers helped themselves and left money on the counter. The supply of flour never ran out, nor did the people eager to buy. By the end of the day, the baker and his wife had enough money to keep their business going.

A rich grocer across the street watched this activity all day wondering what had happened. He asked the couple for their secret.

"No secret," said the baker. "We took a beggar in for the night and in the morning he wished us well and was gone."

The grocer decided that he and his wife must find that beggar and reap a similar reward for their bounty. They found the ragged man quickly enough and rushed him home for a hasty meal and a bed on the floor.

When the beggar left in the morning, he said to the couple, "Whatever you do first, that you will do all day." And with that he was gone.

"Wife," said the grocer, "we have to get ready for all the customers. You sweep the floor and I'll count the change in the till."

And that's what they did, all day long, unable to stop to serve customers, who left in disgust.

Whatever you do first, that you will do all day.

THE PROCESS

I think of this story every morning. Maybe it will help you as it has helped me. I find if I am not strong — and single-minded — my alpha waves will develop leakage. Take this morning. I had intended to get to this book first thing, but first I had to reconfigure my e-mail set-up, which I am finally launching because a provider service is available at last without a long-distance call, and then I wrote a couple of test letters (still glitches), then I wrote a report about The Writers' Union of Canada (TWUC) mentoring program and faxed it, and then I had to send flight information and a brief bio (on file, but always brought up to date) to a host sponsoring me for a reading, and now I have to go to the mailbox and pick up my mail. As I say — leakage.

As you probably already know, there is no such thing as a typical day in the life of a freelance writer. This is at once its joy and its bane. On the one hand, you can prevent burnout because you never do one thing long enough to get sick of it, though sometimes rewrites may bring you to the edge. On the other hand, it's very hard to plan ahead. You'll find yourself constantly doing projections, of money, of course, but also of time. I buy calendars with big spaces in them and then colour-code blocks of time for different activities or deadlines that I must meet. It depends what day it is, what city it is, what time it is, and what's on the agenda, how I figure out a day in the life. Kind of fun. One thing is mandatory: you must not forget your commitments to the people you love and who love you. One thing is guaranteed: you will never be bored.

What you should be is anchored. No matter where you are or what you are doing, familiar work and sleeping habits will keep you sane and organized, if not productive all the time. This is what discipline is all about. You can be creative about your words but not about your routine. Part of mine is early-morning tea and my journal.

I find my journal keeps me sane. It's paper — portable, much lighter than a laptop — and it keeps my finger on reality. I don't use my journal for free-fall; that's for the laptop. A computer gives me a file that can be replicated. My journal, which used to be a wire-bound notebook made of recycled paper but measuring 8.5″ by 11″, is now smaller, a notebook usually measuring 5.5″ by 8″ and fitting, in a pinch, in my handbag. I also now use a Day-Timer appointment book to keep track of my noodges so as to eliminate the imperatives from the daily nag. The old journal has filled several filing cabinet drawers; this new style is threatening to take over cupboards and bookshelves. Isn't storage a drag? Anyway, whatever its form, my journal is my mostly-companion and my paper shrink, but no longer my secretary, noodge, and list-checker. Usually I record the events of the day, a kind of affirmation of what I am doing. But it's there, at the ready, to take complaints and crows, thoughts and doubts, analyses and reactions, reports and plans, editorials and commentary, bleats, and yes, ideas — whatever. Try it.

All writers are told to keep a journal: diary, log, commonplace book, daybook, notebook, workbook, and ubiquitous repository of lists. It doesn't hurt to have several of each, for different purposes and different places. They vary not only from writer to writer but also from day to day and year to year. I find mine range from the depths of banality to the heights of inspiration, acting as buddy, source, release valve, and workbook, depending on my needs and moods. These, as I say, are different from the subconscious dredging that goes on in free-fall, but they're useful on a different level. Here are some other things journals can do:

- Settle arguments, both legal and frivolous; you will have proof of your whereabouts at any given time.
- Justify your expenditures to show the tax man that you aren't making up an account of your activities.
- Win bets.
- Remember names. Because I have such a bad memory for names, I make a point of writing in the full name of someone I have just met, with maybe a thumbnail history or a note of relationships, family, and so on. I rarely go into details about places or things, I suppose because I prefer dialogue to description, but I know lots of writers who do.
- Jog memory. Lillian Hellman commented when she went to write *Pentimento* that while her journal of her trip to Russia was no help at all in what she did record, it was nevertheless useful as a mnemonic and made her recall things she could use.
- Record dialogue. I often write down what people say, either a good line or something I don't understand. Sometimes, later events or discoveries will illuminate an earlier cryptic remark.

I also write in Reminders, Thoughts, Questions, and Nags, marked by arrow icons, which I go back over later and tick off when I've attended to them. Ah, but these are augmented by similar bullets in my engagement calendar and also, now, by slips of paper salvaged from printouts with empty spaces.

If in my journal I am struck by an IDEA, something more than a passing thought, with a brief development of it, I mark it with a Post-It note so I can come back and harvest it later. This is good for what I call Cash Crops — short articles or essays for quick sale to a magazine or newspaper. Sometimes these have come in handy when I'm short of grocery money. The point is, keep a journal.

After that one unwavering ritual of tea-and-journal, I'm easy. Sufficient unto each day is the workload thereof. Actually, it's often more than sufficient, it's overload. You may be writing, marketing, promoting, pitching, filing, reading, interviewing, researching, studying, thinking, clustering, gathering, schmoozing, as well as simply talking, consulting, lecturing, workshopping, conferencing, phoning, mailing — whatever. It's all part of the writing life. How do you make sense of it all as a business? I'll get to business next, but this welter of activity has to be defined and controlled if you're going to survive.

Keep a notebook. Keep several. I'm not talking journal now. Keep what I call seed beds. After all, you have all that paper that you love so well. Fill the seed beds with words, notes, observations, ideas, images, yes, and pictures, drawings, or photographs that mean something to you.

A Case History

Before I wrote *Boy in a Cage*, my chamber opera inspired by my brain-damaged son, Matthew, I found I was collecting images relating to the idea. The original image came from Matt. I had taken him at age six to see a children's play of mine, *Kingsayer*, at the Manitoba Theatre Centre. When he came home he said he liked the "boy in a cage" best, referring to one scene in which a minor character, a playground bully, had been briefly confined to an invisible prison. Behind the continuing action of the play, this actor spent his entrapment miming the flat walls of an invisible barrier. Matthew, himself trapped in an invisible prison, saw this and commented.

Images and ideas for a trapped boy began to accumulate from that time. I found an illustration in a magazine of a head with a wicker cage for a skull; another one, an aerial view of a man caught in a maze of glass and mirrored walls. I taped these pictures in a seed-bed book, one of several blank notebooks I keep for newspaper items, scribbled ideas, seeds that quiver and germinate when I first encounter them, promising to sprout. Similarly, when I went to write my children's

play *The Old Woman and the Pedlar*, I found that I had
a sheaf of images from the germinated seeds all ready to
be gathered into the work I had scarcely been aware was
in progress: notes on noise, wordplay, theatrical tricks,
all related. I recognized what had happened and, trusting the process, have been a ragtag collector ever since.

You can do it, too. The best thing about this particular aspect of
collecting is that it gives you a place to put things you don't know
where to put.

You will find there's a subterranean channel flowing inside you that
picks up words, ideas, images, bits and pieces floating in your sea — the
Jungian stream we all dip into to find: a little paper boat carrying a one-
legged tin soldier, a stray twig of thought, an old leaf dropped from a
tree or a book, all swirling in the eddies of your mind. You know by now
that you're an oyster, always working at some level on a creative irrita-
tion, a pearl of an idea, a seed. A kind of clustering activity is going on
constantly in your subconscious. This is why Brande's dipping and
Mitchell's free-fall are so useful, to throw out the net and bring up
what's accumulating.

RESEARCH

Research is something else, much more conscious and deliberate than
seed-bed germination. You have to know several things about research:
how to conduct it and when to stop, among other things. Actually, first
you have to know what you're looking for. To know that, you should have
at least a preliminary outline, albeit subject to change. It pays to be specific. No sense looking for a needle in the haystack if you're barking up the
wrong haystack. Knowing where to look is the first basic requirement.

The library springs to mind, but these days that's only the beginning, unless you are not on-line. Then you line up for the computers.

Just as I was finishing this book, I went on-line. I was later than many writers because I live in the country and I had to wait for a provider. What bliss! Because the provider was so new, fresh customers were given free hours on the Net between four and seven o'clock in the morning. I did all the research for a big assignment for VISION TV in those wee, large, productive hours, an analysis of the moral obligations of television. Fascinating!

After that it got better and better as I found the rich resources available; I did all the research for my next three books on the Net. Here are two examples of some esoteric knowledge that I found while following keywords.

As you may know, the phrase "conspicuous consumption" was first coined by the American writer Thorstein Veblen (1857–1929). I was able to download Chapter Four of his definitive book, *The Theory of the Leisure Class* (1899), and find an apt quotation from it. That was for my book *Enough.*

For my book *Letters to Icelanders*, I found material on the geothermic substructure of Iceland, on the Icelandic translation of scientific phrases (they refuse to use Greek roots), and on any one of the sagas I cared to explore. These last are not great translations but each chapter of each of the hundreds of sagas is on the Internet and serves to refresh one's memory about the names and events.

Most recently, for the updating of this book, I have followed various links, for example, about lies in non-fiction and about the speedily changing copyright rules regarding reprography and electronic rights. Without leaving my office I have been able to give you fresh URLs, names, and addresses of key players in our profession.

This is not to say that libraries are not valid, they're just a little dated and slower than your electronic servants. No wonder libraries are now called "research resource centres." You'll see students at every computer terminal in every library, catching the information they need for their next term paper. And there are printers and photocopiers ready to put the latest resources into the students' hands to take home and study.

It is impossible to report on this without commenting on the use of resource material and of copying other people's words for your purposes, and I will, in a later chapter. Let me say that I feel about photocopying the way I feel about tape recorders. I believe that taking the time to analyze and select saves hours (and paper!) in the long run and yields more useful files. I mention this here because at the Schlesinger Library at Radcliffe/Harvard, the repository of arguably the most complete women's studies in North America, I did photocopy some delicious pages from Mary McLane's out-of-print, turn-of-the-century diary that I will never be able to buy and own, and I quoted from them (in my book *Reading Between the Lines: The Diaries of Women*), acknowledging my debt in full. (When I sent a copy of the new book with my thanks, I was invited to apply for a research fellowship there if I liked. I liked, but I had other things to do. Pay attention, though: you should always say "thank you.")

In-depth research marks the fiction as well as the non-fiction writer. I used to be awestruck at other writers' knowledge: the names of flowers, or stars, or winds. Michael Ondaatje has two pages about winds in his book *The English Patient*.[5] I remember being overwhelmed by the description of changing a fuse, written by a woman I heard reading at a writers' workshop, and at John Updike's detail of a dentist at work (the different tools on the tray, the neat disposable napkin underneath them). How did these people know so much, how did they remember it all? Research is how. Research, and not taking anything for granted. Always, you have to do your homework, and then you must double-check your facts. Before I asked for permission to use material I found on the Internet, I had to ascertain its authenticity and provenance. One delicious quotation I wanted to use, attributed to a fourteenth-century monk, was impossible to verify, not in my own large reference library, not elsewhere on the Net. I wrote the source directly, asking details about the man and the line, as well as permission to use it, and received no reply, so I didn't use it.

---

5 What's even more fascinating to me, as a writer, are his sources: the *Geographical Journals* of the Royal Geographic Society; a passage from Hassanein Bey's 1923 article about sandstorms, "through Kufra to Darfu," and direct quotations about certain winds from *Heaven's Breath* by Lyall Watson. Research!

So here are a couple of rules about quoting sources: one, don't believe everything you read. Other writers can be careless; you don't have to be. Check your facts, follow up on leads, make sure what you relay is accurate information. Two, remember your manners and your legal obligations. Be sure to acknowledge sources, give credit where credit is due, pay for them if necessary, and always ask permission if you're using a lot of direct quotations or if you are relying heavily on someone else's research or knowledge. If in doubt about something, don't use it. Otherwise, enjoy!

Check your files, too. It helps to have a good backlog of current files, the contents of which you are picking up constantly, building a collection of your own of facts and ideas on subjects that you specialize in, or would like to. Just be careful to document everything you clip, tear, or steal (I'm the one who excises articles and items I need, leaving holes in the magazines in dentists' offices and airplanes.) Write the source and the date at the top of anything you clip, and make sure the name of the writer is clear. Otherwise you have a useless piece of paper, one of those annoying "unnamed sources" that lack credibility. This documentation is particularly important to have when you submit a piece, whether it's an article or a book.

In the case of a magazine assignment, include your sources when you file the story, including names and phone numbers of people you interviewed; for a book, this information often goes into the bibliography, or sometimes into footnotes, but you have to be ready to be challenged by your copy editor. Consider yourself fortunate if you are: smug if you can meet the challenge, and grateful if he/she corrects you before a know-it-all reader brings you up short — and wrong.

In addition to the files of facts and interesting ideas that you cull for yourself, you should, and will, inevitably and inexorably accumulate your own library, specializing in your field(s). This will include reference books, periodicals, various brochures, and other source materials. To keep abreast of information in your field, you should not only subscribe to the relevant magazines but also put yourself on pertinent mailing lists, including e-mail newsletters. You can keep most of these for up to five years, adding new data as it comes in. I clip relevant articles from most magazines but some are so full of information (special issues) that I keep them intact and colour-code stuff I want with Post-It notes.

All of this presents not only a problem in storage but a challenge to file. Like most busy writers, I have a fear of filing. I'm a year behind, usually, not as bad as I used to be, and mostly in the clipping and soft-information area. I'll get to it later — that's what I always say. And eventually I do. Last year I finally managed to go through ALL my files and gave them to the University of Manitoba archives. Then I really felt as if tomorrow were the first day of the rest of my life. But now, a year later, I have to organize the remaining files and work-in-progress and it's daunting again.

The point is, and I do have one, that all this welter, with its backlog of papers and clippings and tear sheets, is as much a part of your writing as your bottom-line four hours a day creating new copy. Reading, remembering, noting, and filing what you need are activities that may not look like writing, but they are a major part of the life. The resources you build are as necessary as your paper and writing equipment. Without them you will have little to say, or at least little or no corroboration.

All you need is space. It's pretty easy to set up a filing system with folders labelled with the topics that interest you. You'll find you have built-in radar for material not only for current projects but also for subjects that fascinate you or that shimmer with possibilities. A once-a-year culling of these is useful if you're running short of space, but waiting longer won't hurt. I have dazzled people (read: editors) with the riches of my files, and will again.

While you're busy putting yourself on mailing lists, give a thought to joining (as soon as you're eligible) some of the professional organizations that may be useful to you, including their newsletters with information about markets, contests, grants, change of personnel in potential customers, and so on. Learn to read with a marker and a cutter so you can save relevant items and toss the rest before you go down in that Dead Sea of paper. This kind of material, of course, goes into different files. You'll probably find it handy to have a current file drawer to keep track of Assignments, Contests & Awards (I've added a folder with months of the year dividers for the deadlines of these), Ideas, Markets, Queries (with a list noting dates of submission and returns), and something I call Targets, which is vaguer but helpful for future possibilities. Add Bookings if you do some public speaking or readings or school workshops.

INTERVIEWS

I must make a specific comment about one particular research technique: the interview, which often poses a dilemma to writers. To tape or not to tape, that is a question a lot of writers ask me. Many journalists swear by tape recorders and say they could not conduct interviews without them. Reporters say that tapes protect them from libel suits when they have recorded evidence to prove their subjects really did say what they are quoted as saying. Novelist Katherine Govier told me that an interview she had recorded with an incest victim was enough for the woman to lay charges against her father even though they came long after the statute of limitations might have rendered her claims invalid, because the testimony was taped before the time had run out. Taped conversations can be used as evidence in court, or used to be, although they are no longer considered as trustworthy as they once were. These days, with our increasing awareness of how sounds and images can be manipulated and massaged — and our increasing skill at doing so — we find it difficult to know what to believe, not hearing, not seeing the actual event.

It's not for legal reasons that I stick to my preference for one-on-one interviews without a tape recorder to come between my subject and me. Taped interviews, frankly, double the work. They also paralyze the writer. With a recorder the writer sits there and chats, trusting an electronic memory. Back at the office, the whole thing has to be done again: the listening, the editing, the note-taking, the condensing, the shaping — work that doubles the time. Trusting a tape, a writer does less editing at the time of the interview and seldom follows up a key point with any sharpness, figuring the subject will get around to it without urging. Without a recorder and with adequate homework beforehand, a writer can accomplish half the writing during the interview. I do.

That homework involves learning something about your subject beforehand. Get the basic background, at least; read relevant material, including a sampling of what this person has written (or performed?), if anything. In other words, be prepared. Don't go in and ask stupid or redundant questions. If you're doing a biographical piece, don't ask for the birth date, spouse's name(s), milestones in the interviewee's career, the reasons for a claim to fame or importance. You should already know all that. Analyze what you need to find out; make a list of questions you want answers to.

In the course of my various kinds of research for various kinds of assignments, I had toyed with the idea of tape but had not succumbed. Then I read Truman Capote's *In Cold Blood*, a breakthrough at the time (1966) in what was called creative non-fiction. Real people became characters in the suspenseful story of the murder of a family by two normal-looking, crazed killers. Capote accomplished amazing verisimilitude — or was it dazzling narrative? — based on his extensive interviews, all done, or so he said, without a tape recorder. The writer, interviewed extensively as the book flew up best-seller lists, explained that he felt that not only a tape recorder but also a notepad came between him and his subjects, so he eschewed both. He added that he had almost total recall. What he did was rush to paper as soon as the interview was over, writing down everything that was said with as much detail as possible.

I tried this when I was doing research for what became *The Horsburgh Scandal* (1976), a play I worked on collectively with Theatre Passe Muraille in Toronto. Reverend Russell Horsburgh was a United Church minister who had been arrested, tried, and convicted of contributing to juvenile delinquency in his church. He actually served about ninety days in prison before the Supreme Court of Canada acquitted him because he had been convicted on the strength of the uncorroborated evidence of juveniles. Anyone who had contact with the man had a strong opinion of him: equally intelligent, reasonable, sane people told me the man was 1) the devil incarnate, or 2) an angel come to earth. Families were split on the decision; the last town the minister lived in was torn apart. Wherever I went and whomever I talked to, no one wanted a pencil to record their vehement views, let alone a machine.

I used Capote's method, running to the car where my notebook was waiting. I'm pretty good at taking notes, no shorthand skills but my own shortcuts learned from years of listening to lectures, and I make comments as I go along. I know a good quotable line when I hear one; I write down a pertinent statement word for word and put quotations marks around it so I know these are my subject's own words. By the time I go to write up the interview, half my writing is already done. That to me is the advantage of paper over tape. In any case, that material was destined for drama, so I didn't have to be word-for-word accurate. What I needed to evoke was the essence of the emotions.

The real test of my interviewing skills came for me when the United Church of Canada commissioned me to do a collection of interviews with twenty different people from across Canada, covering as varied a range of age, gender, occupation, and social status as possible (*No Two Alike*). The angle of the book was the illumination of each person's spiritual journey, catching a soul on a path, as it were.

A committee helped me select the people from taped background interviews, so that I learned something of them ahead of time, enough to enable me to decide who should be included. In order to ensure cross-country representation, I added a couple of people I knew of or was told about, with no such background material to help. I made my appointments and proceeded to travel to meet my subjects. At best, I had twenty-four hours with each of them, but not consecutive or unbroken time, just over dinner and maybe some time the next day — church on Sunday, or breakfast — once as an overnight guest. At the least, I had the length of time of one interview lasting an hour or two, sometimes a little longer. I had to use the time well.

When I was ready to write, I took all my papers with me to Bermuda where I had friends who offered me a place to work in return for taking care of their basset hounds. (They found it cheaper to feed me than to put their dogs in a kennel when they went off the island.) I also took along Strunk & White, and Zinsser (see Suggested Reading) and wrote the twenty interviews. I never had to call anyone for additional information or corrections. I had it all.

As for the interviewing itself, as with any kind of probe you conduct into another person or behaviour, you need several different attributes, not all of them terribly virtuous qualities but useful for a writer. To get a good interview here is what you need:

- the friendliness of a puppy
- the eagerness of a gossip
- the lust of a lover
- the nose of a detective
- the energy of a five year old
- the faith of a mother
- the cynicism of a reporter
- the trust of a dog
- the passion of a convert
- the naïveté of a tourist

You are, after all, travelling in a strange country and you have a lot to learn about this landscape. Your subject will probably never realize how much you know. That's why, in the case of *No Two Alike*, I insisted that each of my subjects receive a copy of his or her profile to make sure I didn't reveal anything too private; this was, after all, a soul report. The real point is that tapes never record what people don't say.

You know that when you listen to people, you have to listen to what they're really saying, or not saying, as the case may be. I have a friend who always uses a certain phrase before she tells me something that makes her angry. She says, "I have to laugh," or "It makes me laugh," and then she tells the tale of neglect or folly that has outraged her. (Until very recently, most women had never been permitted anger; they had to laugh.) I mention this tag here because it's another source of information that a writer must notice and use. Such a conversational tic is especially valuable for a playwright and for any writer who deals in dialogue. All writers have to listen between the lines, not with a tape but with the heart.

Putting It Together

So far I've been dealing with the gathering of your resources and strengths, part of the ongoing activity of any day in the life of a writer, necessary but pointless without an intended use. You're stockpiling your cupboard, is all; now you have to figure out how to use the contents.

On one shelf you have your skills. Now you've added your subjects, all the topics you specialize in and the ideas you would like to pursue. You have something to say and the means to say it. Now you have to figure out how to make the two commodities pay off. Take a look at your options:

- **Fiction writing:** short stories; books; mysteries, thrillers, romances, plus more so-called serious work ("literature"); children's stories and books;
- **Biography:** really non-fiction but includes ghostwriting, life writing, memoirs, guest-editing;
- **Non-fiction writing:** magazine and newspaper articles including book reviews, reviews, reports, profiles, interviews, and investigative journalism; familiar (as opposed to academic) essays; self-help; how-to; business; history; *belles lettres*; humour; newsletters; business reports;
- **Drama:** radio plays, stage plays; feature-film screenplays; children's theatre; puppet plays; play therapy;

- **Television:** reports; documentaries; docudramas; MOWs (Movie of the Week); children's shows; animated stories;
- **Poetry:** lyrics, light verse; jingles; epic, narrative; and
- **Speaking:** guest lectures; readings; seminars; workshops; teaching; ghostwriting speeches.

I spoke to a playwright who was hard-pressed, short of cash between productions and grants. I suggested she write an article or two for a theatre-arts magazine or a more popular one for a general or women's magazine and she blanched and whispered, "I can't!" I could never afford such selectivity.

If you plan to take the plunge as a freelancer, be prepared to think of all the ways your skill with words can help you earn a living. You may dream of writing the Great Canadian Novel or a hit play, but such an aspiration won't put food on your table. You need to consider a broad range of types of work. Some you'll enjoy more than others; some will pay better than others; some will be easier; and some, you will realize, you aren't suited to at all (like me with ghostwriting). You are a salesperson. What do you have to sell?

- Your grammatical and language skills may serve you in extreme need or early days, by enabling you to proofread or correct copy or rewrite other people's work.
- If your first love is drama, does your ear for dialogue or your sense of voice enable you to put words in other people's mouths — on paper, as in ghostwriting, or literally, as in speech-writing?
- Are there communication needs in your subject area that you could fill? I know several versatile non-fiction writers who write business and annual reports for large firms, which pay more handsomely than *belles lettres*. So does government, many departments of which farm out reports, surveys, programs, and brochures for freelancers to write. Be warned: government offices are notoriously so slow to pay that they have long since institut-

ed interest payments on overdue accounts, comforting when the cheque arrives, but don't hold your breath or waste it complaining about this waste of taxpayers' money.

- Can you talk as well as write? Most, though not all, writers can. If you can, you can parlay your skill with words into peripheral activities like (keynote) speech-making in your area of expertise, conducting workshops or seminars, reading (from your own work), and talking on radio or television (panels, talk shows, your own material, expert advice), all of which pay varying amounts of money depending on your reputation, expertise, and the subject matter. As soon as you qualify, it will pay you to join the Writers' Guild of Canada (WGC), the writers' spin-off from the Alliance of Canadian Cinema, Television & Radio Artists (ACTRA), which helps to guarantee you a minimum fee scale. Check with the local office and find out what the requirements are for membership.
- Consider, by all means, other forms than the genre of your choice. Build from what you know, capitalizing on some interest or expertise in one area and go on from there.

I met a poet who writes for a television series. I know a travel writer who writes business reports, and a playwright who writes cookbooks (me). I know a mystery writer who writes book reviews and a poet who writes social history. I can think of three playwrights who write humour. I know a novelist who writes memoirs. I met an academic who writes plays under a different name, and I heard of another one who writes mysteries, also with a pseudonym. I went to a writers' workshop with a serious novelist who writes romances (different name). I know one composer and one lyricist who write kids' TV shows. I can name you any number of writers who perform their own work: stand-up comedy, performance pieces, one-handers. I worked with a screenwriter who teaches. As a matter of fact, a lot of writers become part-time teachers, most frequently in the summer, conducting workshops and seminars at summer art camps or community colleges.

One thing leads to another. Sometimes your range of subject matter broadens and develops; sometimes you acquire other skills, picking things up as you go along. When it comes to subject matter, begin, of course, with what you know.

Write about what you know. Writers are told that all the time; it's taken to mean that if you are a homemaker in Winnipeg you don't try to write about life on the Left Bank in Paris and — more political these days, re voice appropriation — if you're a white college-grad bank teller, you're not supposed to try to get inside the head of an aboriginal activist. Like that. But when I started, I wasn't creating voices or imagining strange milieus. I was trying to make a buck. I needed to sell information that I already knew or at least that was close at hand and that wasn't going to cost me much in time, travel, or effort to gather. I turned to non-fiction, that is, to newspapers and magazines, as I assessed my wares and figured out where to peddle them.

I remember something my husband told me when he was in the advertising business. He said he always had to find his client's Point of Difference. Lots of people sold bread; what was the PoD that made the bread he was selling more attractive to the buyer? Convenience? Freshness? Taste? Seven grains? (Not in those days!) So now I asked myself: What did my words have that others did not? What did I know that others didn't?

I knew the Stratford Festival, the workings thereof, on stage and off. I decided that's what I would try to sell first. Bearing all this in mind, take a look at a brief history of the first pieces I sold. (This was in 1973; you'll probably notice that fees have not changed much since then, not as much as the cost of bread or rent.)

1) A careful analysis of the cuts and emendations to *Pericles*, playing at the Festival that summer. An editor with *The Shakespearean Newsletter*, out of Chicago, had expressed an interest in a query. I wrote the piece and sent it and never heard from him again, not even a free copy. However, a scholarly

friend of mine saw my byline and commented, so I know the essay was published. Income zero, not even tear sheets.

2) An interview with Polly Bohdanetsky, jewelry maker at the Festival that summer, about her designs for the production of *Macbeth*. This piece was published by an American magazine called *Northwestern Jeweller*, and I was paid $19 American for it. My first interview!

3) A piece on the uses and application of computer technology to theatre needs, devised by my husband. He was among the first to use attendance projections to help plan programming; to keep a close, informed watch on invoices to track and control production expenses; to set up an adumbration of Ticketron for seat sales. There was no in-house computer; figures were driven weekly to a terminal in Guelph for analysis and implementation. My report of these cutting-edge applications appeared in a new computer magazine published in the East. (Silicon Valley didn't exist then, nor did silicone chips.) I was paid $60 American. Coming right along.

4) Heartened by all this, I offered *Canadian Motorist* (later *Leisureways*, now *Journey*, the magazine still published by the Canadian Automobile Association) a sparkling piece about a weekend at Stratford — theatre for tourists. The editor said no. What he did want was a sparkling piece about a weekend in the Muskokas. I phoned the manager of the Muskoka summer theatre who lived in Gravenhurst. I was still in Stratford. We agreed to meet in Toronto, about equidistant for each of us. I got my story and a new friend, and was paid $150 Canadian. I had some expenses (gas to Toronto) but Michael Cole bought lunch. The ethics of this never occurred to me.

I must report that the successor to my husband's job, when he found out that I planned to write about the theatre, did two things for me: one, arranged interviews and access to up-to-date information about the theatre; two, paid me a bonus of $25 every time I got the Stratford Festival into print. I don't think he really considered it a valuable form of advertising; I think he was trying to slip a little extra money in my purse. I was grateful at the time, also naïve. I see it now as unethical. My friend was actually buying my pen (typewriter). I wouldn't do it now, partly because I don't need the money so desperately and mostly because I know better.

During this time of apprenticeship, spending a lot of juice on my assignments, I was also struggling with life as a fresh, raw widow, a single mother, and a worried breadwinner. The then-editor-in-chief (later publisher) of the *Toronto Star* was a friendly acquaintance and gave me my first professional advice and encouragement. He was the first to suggest I move to Toronto for the work and opportunities. He was also the first person to offer me a job, saying, "There's a little paper in Toronto that might buy your work," and in fact it did, a short piece about my fresh widowhood. I wonder now if anyone has to move, what with e-mail, faxes, the Internet, and so on. However, there's still a lot to be said for schmoozing, which is still done face-to-face.

In any case, my little piece, plus an article I read in *Maclean's* magazine by a divorced man about life as a single male (learning how to vacuum, shop, and so on) spurred me to offer an expanded article on widowhood to the national magazine, still a monthly general at that time. I knew the then-editor Peter Newman slightly, having met him at Festival openings. He gave me a go-ahead but cautioned me to "make it as witty as you can."

Jane Austen once said, "People who do not complain are seldom pitied." So I didn't complain; I was wry but not watery. Not only was I eloquent — I was, after all, writing about what I knew, or at least was learning rapidly, first-hand — I also strummed a chord in others. The mail poured in.

An avalanche of personal letters addressed or forwarded to me tumbled into my mailbox and a similar load fell on the magazine. I was never told officially, but I learned a few years later from a former editor that the volume of mail received in response to my article was the biggest readership reaction in the history of the magazine up to that time. I may not have known that, but I did realize that I was on to something big.

I approached a book publisher suggesting a book about widowhood. This was just after Lynne Caine had published her book *Widow* in the United States and hit the best-seller lists. The publisher told me that while I wrote "like an angel" and certainly made her fear for her husband's life, nevertheless, when you'd read one widow you'd read them all, so forget it. I almost did. But then an ad account executive who had seen my piece in *Maclean's* invited me to expand on it, to write a series of brochures about widowhood for his client, the Canadian Life Insurance Association (later the Canadian Life and Health Insurance Association — CLHIA). I was given an expense account to help me with my research, plus access to people in the industry to teach me what I needed to know about life insurance along with a smattering of financial advice.

By this time, two years after my husbands' death, I had moved to Toronto, having spent too many tiring hours on Highway 401 between the city and Stratford and having undergone major surgery for bleeding ulcers. With no money, no friends in town, no strength, and no contacts, I had nowhere to go but up.

Writing the brochures was like a catharsis for me. I used technical and statistical information from the books and material I could afford to buy on that generous expense account, as well as from interviews arranged for me, but I also drew from my own gut reactions recorded in the diary I had begun to keep within hours of my husband's death. I had a complete, accurate record of my recovery, if you can call it that. Trauma is a better word. When the powers at the insurance association looked at my material they rejected it as a kit and opted for a book, saying, moreover, that I was free to negotiate it with a publisher, with a built-in guarantee of sales. This time the publisher was interested.

Beginnings: A Book for Widows was published in the fall of 1977 and has been in print every since. It has been updated four times, the latest being the twentieth-anniversary edition in the spring of 1997, and each time I have added later nuggets of painfully acquired wisdom. The emotional story has never changed. It has been published in the United States, Great Britain, Australia, New Zealand, and South Africa, and in large print. Until 1995 CLHIA kept buying large numbers of copies for its member insurance companies to purchase at cost and use as a tool at their discretion. London Life, for example, gave away a copy of the book with every death claim it settled, and continues to do so.

Women who read the book have seldom been widowed for more than three years, often closer to three months; some are still bleeding around the eyes. Wherever I go publicly, wherever I speak, whatever my subject, two or three widows will come to talk to me about *Beginnings* and they start by saying, "You saved my life." And I know who they are. They bring dog-eared first editions for me to sign and tell me how many people they've lent their copy to, but they always make a point of getting it back. I wish I had a nickel for every time the book has been loaned, returned, and loaned again. I can't complain, however; over the years the book and its spin-offs have been my biggest single moneymaker. I have become, I say wryly and ruefully, a professional widow.

This experience taught me about spin-offs, that is, speeches, talks, workshops, short stuff, that is, other sources of income for related services. For a while I was the darling of the insurance industry because I was a (fairly) young widow, a perfect example of how not to back into widowhood. I didn't mind; if I was being exploited, at least I was being paid well. I felt that I was using the industry to reach other women like myself who didn't have a clue about finances or survival. Everything I learned I learned the hard way and then, Sunday-school teacher that I was, I had to pass on my lessons to others.

This led me eventually to write, with an old buddy from Winnipeg, Lynne Macfarlane, a book of financial planning for women called *Everywoman's Money Book* (five updated revised editions, the last one published in 1995) and, by myself, *The Best Is Yet to Come: Planning a Financially Secure Retirement*. This one, after one revision, was dropped for a while and then re-sold and updated (1996) and rewritten with another partner, Christopher Cottier, with the same title except *planning* was replaced by *enjoying*.

I tell you all this in detail because it is a practical illustration of how you can sell your acquired and accumulated knowledge and hard-won experience. My late husband always used to say if you get a lemon, make lemonade. I parlayed my lemons into a career and it's still going on. Because of those books and the profile I had forged as a female financial expert, I was invited onto the Mutual Funds Board of Investors' Group of Canada, later subsumed into the Investors' Group Trust Board, from which I finally retired in 2001. Later, I was asked to be the narrator-host of a thirteen-part television series, "Women, Lifestyle and Money," which was my idea originally, but only as a writer. Produced in 1995, it will keep turning up on cable for a few years.

The moral to this long story is that you never know where your next dollar is coming from and it never pays to say no to anything — almost never. Thus, from widowhood to financial planning for women to generic retirement planning to a concern for the family, and for the elderly, one thing led to another. My interest in women and in their expression of grief in diaries led me to a deep examination of women's journals and life-writing, and another book, *Reading Between the Lines: The Diaries of Women* (Key Porter Books). I wrote a book about my brain-damaged son; a one-man play and a chamber opera were also inspired by Matthew; and now I'm working on a movie based on an incident in his life. I also discovered the most menial writing I could do when he fell into madness and I was his keeper during his recovery. I "wrote" brochures for Wintario — more like copied. Even minimal grammatical corrections were frowned on as being too creative.

Much of my investigative journalism into the hidden lives of disadvantaged people has surfaced in other forms, in plays and poetry. Always I have been driven by an intensely personal interest as well as by my need to survive. You can do that, too. The world is still an oyster up for grabs and the pearl may be as close as your next assignment.

CONFIDENCE OR IGNORANCE?

Everyone's case history is unique but perhaps you can learn a few things from mine, things I learned slowly and with increasing awe of my chosen craft.

When I was first married, my husband refused to eat liver, which I loved. He agreed to try it a dozen times if I would cook it a different way each time I served it. Being young, academic, and certainly not a cook, I didn't know there were twelve ways to cook liver. I took cookbooks out of the library, because I owned only one, and began to experiment. One of the twelve ways was a soufflé. I was too uninformed to know that soufflés were difficult. Full of heavy minced liver, my soufflé rose like a daydream. Bill didn't like it, but that's not the point. If you don't think about the difficulties involved, but go ahead and tackle the problem, chances are you'll succeed. You will certainly learn something. So with writing.

Every time I was given an assignment, I pretended that I could do it. If I didn't know how to do it, I would learn. That's what books are for, to teach you, and also people, also trial and error. Initially I had time. I could spend three weeks polishing two thousand words. I made up in time and assiduous attention what I lacked in skill and efficiency. Like Saint Peter walking on the water, I knew I could do it if I kept my eyes on the goal. The trick is not to look down, or back.

People will keep trying to say no to you. Don't take no for an answer; don't even expect it, not from others, not from yourself. There are different kinds of no, and you have to deal with all of them.

First, in landing the assignment, don't discourage yourself or others. You have to assume that *of course* you are going to get the job, because *of course* you are the best person for it, and *of course* you can do it, never mind (and don't bother telling your prospective client) that you've never written a profile before, or a travel piece, or a documentary film. You'll figure it out.

Then you have to brace yourself for the barrelful of negatives that your editor dumps all over you. This may be annoying but it's helpful in the long run. You have to believe that this nitpicker and you have a common goal: the clearest, best expression that you are capable of. Take the criticism seriously. At the same time, you have to obey your own instincts. I remember my examining board criticizing something facetious I had written in my M.A. thesis, warning me that when I was older I would regret it. I refused to cut the offending paragraph (it was a poem, actually), and I have never regretted it. Always remember that a lot of writing is editing. You'll have to learn to be your own best editor.

The third, most devastating no you can't afford to pay too much attention to is the thumb-down signal you may get from critics. How do you deal with it/them? Some writers (performers, too) simply ignore it, refusing to read criticism of their work. Others read it and suffer. Not that it doesn't hurt, but you have to find a way to learn what you can, if there is indeed anything to learn, and then to assert yourself, your belief in your work, and go on.

> In the movie about the artist Van Gogh (I didn't see it, but the actor William Hutt described this scene to me, for obvious reasons), a critic came to see the painter's work, scrutinized the paintings briefly and then dismissed them all by saying, "You paint too fast." Angry, Van Gogh replied, "You *look* too fast!"

Most critics do look too fast. Just as I am picky about the brains I pick to help me, so I am picky about the critics whose words I will take to heart — no, not to heart, because they all pierce — to mind. Remember the old line about those who can, do; those who can't, teach. Is the logical conclusion that those who can neither do nor teach, criticize? I'd like to say it is, but then I would be depriving writers of a source of income. Lots of writers I know, including me, write book and theatre reviews. The most obvious advice I have to give here is: read the book. (A lot of reviewers don't.)

These negatives are obstacles that you, as a writer, must overcome. The bad news is that they will continue as long as you write. The good news is that you develop a philosophical attitude about the "tall poppy syndrome" that characterizes a lot of Canadian critics: the tendency to lop the heads off any poppies that dare to grow above the crowd. You will also build up keloid tissue, a thick skin, and, conversely, a sensitivity to others' pain. Sticks and stones break bones, it is true, but words can leave indelible scars.

A few more thoughts about your time and effort.

PARABLE

An irate patient went to his doctor to protest the bill he had received for the relief of a dislocated shoulder. "All you did," he said, "was look at my shoulder and pull it once. Why does that cost $100?" The doctor answered by breaking down the costs of the services rendered. "For what you call pulling your shoulder: $5. For knowing where to pull: $95."

My doctor-father used to say that as he grew older in his profession he made up in expertise what he had initially lacked in experience, so that most cases took less time to treat. So with you. You may start slowly, spending a lot of juice and energy on your first assignments, probably more than they are worth. But you're in a training period and you will have to go slowly as you learn lessons you won't forget. As time goes on and your confidence and skill grow, you will be able to knock off a piece in much less time than it used to take. This is not to say you don't treat it with respect; you just have a better idea of what you're doing. When you reach this stage, don't, repeat *do not*, give a job more care and attention than it deserves. If you do, you're cheating yourself of income.

You simply can't afford to spend two weeks on a $200 quickie of nine hundred words.

I had a cousin who prided herself on her sewing skill and the care she took in her work. She considered it admirable to give as much time and attention to the darning of a dishrag as to the invisible mending of a fine silk blouse. This is a waste of effort. Don't you do it. Assess your job before you start and figure out roughly how much time it should take and therefore how much you will earn from it per hour.

Years ago when a new play of mine was opening out of town (in a small city in Iowa), the Chamber of Commerce invited me to be the lunch speaker talking about the business of playwriting. I had never actually counted how much time I spent on a play. It took a while but I finally came up with a figure for a complete production-ready manuscript, from moment of inception, through rewrites, discussions, readthroughs, rehearsals, and fine-tuning, not counting my paper or postage. I earned about twenty-seven cents an hour. What, and quit showbiz?

OCCUPATIONAL HAZARDS

"Looks like De Quervain's to me," said a woman to me several years ago, from across a crowded plane. She was right and I was astonished, but not for long. Turned out she worked for a workers' compensation board and was familiar with the various forms of Repetitive Strain Injury (RSI) being reported on claims. For our different reasons both of us were slightly ahead of the present acute awareness of the debilitating damage and chronic pain accompanying a number of different ailments I couldn't even spell before I got mine. Besides my De Quervain's Syndrome, there are tendonitis, tenosynovitis, epicondylitis, and Carpal Tunnel Syndrome (CTS) — the last the most common if there is a mouse in the house.

Busy writers used to get some form of RSI but they called it writers' cramp. Louisa May Alcott, best remembered for *Little Women*, called herself a "writing machine" and wrecked her thumb and arm with the pressure of making carbon copies. She took laudanum or morphine for the pain, tried massage, "electricity," and "letting divine strength flow in" as possible cures, but nothing worked. Eventually she had to reduce her writing time and productivity.

The aggravating pain and irritating delays caused by his aching wrist and fingers forced the prolific American novelist Henry James to resort to dictation — directly to a keyboard, by way of an amanuensis (court stenographer?). There are no reports of RSI among his successive employees.

Today, RSI injuries affect all kinds of workers: dental hygienists, telephone and jackhammer operators, carpenters, musicians, postal clerks, food-service employees, hair stylists, cashiers, all office staff who use computers — and writers. And women seem to be more at risk than men. No one has produced specific figures yet, but there's no dearth of dire predictions and projections; the basic fact is that ten times as many RSIs as there were ten years ago have cost the economy between $20 to 100 billion a year and account for more time lost than amputations or fractures. Writers have to take the problem seriously. It truly is an occupational hazard.

My excuse for my troubles, murmured to people who questioned the ugly fiberglass splint taped with dirty, fraying Velcro that I wore on my left wrist for almost two years was: "Old injury, new computer." I had broken my wrist in a fall three years earlier, a simple Colley's fracture from which I had recovered fully, having faithfully performed all my physio homework and rehab exercises. I had thought I was back to working strength until, two years after the fall, I acquired a new laptop computer and added three hours a day to my already full workload at the desktop. The increased strain was more than a taxed tendon could bear. Suddenly I was in constant pain.

Muscle relaxants merely masked the symptoms and made me nauseous. A shot of silicone hurt like hell and didn't do any good. A long-term course of ultrasound plus ice packs plus gentle exercises plus that ugly custom-made splint slowly, slowly had some effect, along with a thorough analysis of my working habits and facilities, which is why I'm telling you this now. If you want to avoid such pain, inconvenience, and potential loss of income through disability, you must pay attention to your physical surroundings and well-being. If you plan on writing four or more hours a day, especially at a computer, note the following.

The operator — that's you, the writer — must sit up straight in front of the keyboard, with the monitor in front of that, not off to the side. You need a firm, upright back support on an armless chair, feet flat on the floor or on a footrest, thighs parallel to the floor. The keyboard should be at elbow height so that your arms are parallel to your thighs and your hands neither raised, lowered, nor stretched to reach the keys. Touch typists should not stretch for the farther keys, but move their hands; two-finger wonders should vary the use of their fingers. I used to recommend a wrist rest but am told now that your wrists are better off "floating." I just got a gel pad! Use the keyboard commands as much as you can to avoid the use of the mouse, no matter what kind it is, and rest your hands in your lap instead of on the mouse while waiting for a program or something to come up. Make sure the screen of the monitor is about arm's length away from you, with the top of it level with your eyes.

You can get a computer program that clicks in regularly and reminds you to take a stretch break, but that's expensive. The Net is full of exercises and stretch programs designed to keep you supple and free of pain. I've provided a URL in the Appendix that links many RSI-related Web sites. The warm-up exercises for tai chi are great for wrists and arms, also for breathing. Don't forget to breathe. The trouble is, of course, that one does forget — to breathe deeply, to stretch regularly, to relax deeply, and to stop intermittently. Fifteen minutes are gone in the blink of an eye, an hour ditto, when you're deep in alpha waves.

As for my laptop, I have arranged a support under my left (weak) arm when I write in the La-Z-Boy. I tried not to forget to wear my splint when I wrote, but it was a relief when I didn't need to any more.

Not until the pain was upon me did I take positive steps to alleviate it. People are advised now to take those steps as preventive measures, a far more effective approach. Of course, since I am self-employed, I couldn't take any time off with pay; I had to keep working. I understand now that after a staggering payout in compensation for a work-related injury, computer companies are doing their best to slough off the blame. In my case, once the worst had passed I was determined to keep ahead of the problem. If I'd stayed much longer on ultrasound I'd have been classified as chronic and then the treatment would not have been included in my medical insurance. As it was, the forty-five-minute drive each way, and the gas (and time) it cost, came out of my pocket. I still have to favour my left thumb and wrist, being careful how I carry parcels or luggage or a cup and saucer, how I hold an apple when I peel it, how I open a door or a bottle of wine. I am constantly amazed at how much pressure is required by the other hand when I think I'm doing all the work with the corkscrew. Wrist splints are no help as a preventive tool, by the way, and offer meager comfort to people who must keep working while already suffering. Few, indeed, can afford to stop what they do for a living.

One thing I wanted to avoid, if I could help it, was surgery. Knives are drastic and there's no going back. I actually went for an examination by a surgeon who, it seemed, specialized in these scrape, cut, or tuck jobs and who urged me to call him if/when it got too bad. I carried his card in my wallet for months as a reminder — or as a threat — so I would behave myself.

Look up RSI on the Internet. You'll find cautionary tales, exercises, several newsletters, and more advice than you can absorb in one sitting. You shouldn't be sitting there, anyway. You will be warned to go easy on the Net, cool it on the e-mail, and stay away from computer games. There goes Free Cell! Books abound, however (you'll ruin your eyes!). Try to go for natural aids: steam, both hot and dry (sauna); yoga; tai chi; and massage — nice if that last comes with TLC, but don't count on it. Your need will wear out even the most patient of unpaid caregivers.

Watch your eyes as well. As a reader and a writer, you must take care of them. If you already require corrective lenses then you must adjust them to the screen. I was aware of this problem long before I had my RSI. For my first computer I measured the space between my eyes and the screen and then had my prescription for that distance made up into granny glasses with a large lens area. If I wear them to walk across the room, I'll fall down. With this aid I can write for eight to twelve hours a day without a headache in sight.

I keep these glasses in the desk drawer beside the computer and must remember to take them with me on any trip with the laptop. Once, in the old days when I was still going on retreat to write, I forgot my special glasses, found it impossible to wave my head up and down using my bifocals and settled for writing with the naked eye. I developed a headache that lasted for three days after I returned home. So you be careful. Get out your tape measure. You must be ergonomically responsible. The word *ergonomics* is in the supplement to the *Oxford English Dictionary*. Derived from the Greek *ergon*, it means "the scientific study of the efficiency of man in his working environment." Woman, too.

According to *Lancet* magazine, cited by the OED, a group of people decided in 1950 to form an organization called the Ergonomics Research Society. In 1952, in the Oxford *Mail*, K.F.H. Murrell reported that he had found it necessary to invent the word *ergonomics* to describe the work he and others were doing, studying work in relation to environment. By 1961, the keyboard had been ergonomically designed to make every key more accessible to typists' fingers. You've probably seen some of these designs with their intriguing contours and angles and prices. By 1969, the *London Times* reported a new car seat designed by the ergonomics department of a car manufacturer. In 1970, ergonomics had become the focus of industrial psychologists and work physiologists analyzing work absenteeism. You are not alone in paying attention to your bod.

Give a thought, while you're at it, to that old keyboard. We all know by now that the QWERTY keyboard was deliberately arranged to slow people's fingers so that the keys wouldn't jam on their way to the paper.

As the machinery became more efficient, a new keyboard was designed, but most typewriters were committed to the old one by their manufacturers, and business colleges still taught the old configuration in their touch-typing courses. When computers were introduced into offices, it was possible to create one's own keyboard through the decisive use of macros, but I never heard of anyone who bothered. I am told that an experienced typist can learn the new keyboard within two weeks to a month, but I never tried. I know a lot of writers who don't type, that is, touch-type; icons were made for them. These are older people. If you're just starting out, perhaps it would pay you to learn to type with all your fingers. It would boost your production and efficiency — and you can learn the best keyboard without preconditioned reflexes. Computer companies have been experimenting with different keyboard designs, splitting them, changing their position to vertical, and so on.

You can keep on working as long as your fingers stay supple and your eyes stay clear. If they do eventually seize up or cloud over, as the case may be, do not despair. Voice-activated computers are getting cheaper all the time. The great thing about freelance writing is that you'll never have to retire. May God grant you your marbles.

PART FIVE

The Writing Business

*In Which the Writer Considers Money,
the Making Thereof, the Work, and the Pitfalls*

To Market, To Market

Now that you have some idea of what you can write and what you can write about, you have to figure out where to sell it. Do I have to tell you not to submit to *The New Yorker* or *Atlantic Monthly* for starters? Mind you, right off the top I can think of three Canadian writers who did and sold their first stories to those prestigious markets. Who am I to say? Anyway, those were fiction pieces. Your best bet as a freelancer seeking fast income is non-fiction in a field you know, to a market you can handle (badger) and turn into a regular customer.

Sooner or later, preferably sooner, you will realize the huge role that marketing plays in your life. You can have all the ideas in the world and you can be a writing machine, but if you don't sell what you write, where are you? I spend 30 percent of my time just peddling my product, my wares, my self, and even more when I'm between assignments and anxious for work. You need to hustle to keep on getting work; to get work, you have to query. The main thing to remember about queries is that you are trying to get an editor's attention.

PARABLE

Once upon a time Farmer A sold a donkey to Farmer B, assuring him that the donkey was amenable and would do anything it was told. On the strength of that promise, Farmer B bought the donkey and took it home. A week later he was back complaining.

"You said that donkey would do anything I said," he shouted. "Well, it doesn't. I want my money back."

Farmer A looked at B calmly and told him to watch. Then he took a two-by-four and went up to the donkey and raised the two-by-four and went WHOCK! right between its eyes.

"Move!" he shouted.

> The poor beast blinked and lurched into action and Farmer A explained: "You just have to get the donkey's attention."

That's what you're doing with a query, getting the donkey's attention.

Shortly after I turned pro, I read a short article on good business correspondence that had a long-lasting effect on my epistolary life. It's this: always begin a letter with *you*. I've done it ever since, and I tell all my students to do the same. This applies to personal as well as business letters, although it seems to disappear in e-mail.

People are always more interested in themselves than they are in you. When you begin your letter by telling them how you feel and what you want, they won't be nearly as intrigued as if you start by telling them something they want to hear — about themselves. The brief pause you take to shift the pronoun from *I* to *you* forces you to consider the recipient's goals and to rethink yours. You might decide your idea isn't good enough, or that you don't know enough yet to write it. You might also come up with a better angle. Think about it.

Try something like "Your magazine has always been intriguing (provided it isn't only two issues old!), or "You're a busy person but never too busy to hear a new idea ..." You can also demonstrate while you're at it that you know what the magazine has been featuring lately: "Your recent series on brass widgets has been fascinating. Did you know ...?" — but only if you can hit the editor with a new angle or a spin-off that only you can do and suggest a piece as a follow-up.

Starting with *you* not only puts your target in your sights, it also makes you think of what that person wants. You know what you want: you want to sell an idea, get an assignment, and make some money. What do your editors, your potential employers want? All of them want to keep filling their magazines, newspapers, newsletters, etc., with well-written, well-researched, interesting material to hold their readership and to increase it.

Your first task is to convince them that you are the one to help them achieve those goals. You do this by writing a neat, accurate, well-spelled (for heaven's sake, spell the editor's name correctly!) letter, citing your expertise and relevant experiences, mentioning some early pertinent publication(s) and demonstrating, as I say, your familiarity with the publication and your assessment of its audience. Your lead is very important, as is the opening paragraph. In fact, it may be the lead of your story when you write it.

This approach applies to book publishers and play or movie producers as well. If you know of any reasons your book/play/creation should sell, any special audience appeal (being sure that you know the audience and the approach of the potential client), then spell them out. Suggest special sale possibilities in the case of a publisher, or unique audiences to a producer, in addition, of course, to the universal appeal of your subject and writing skill.

It takes a certain amount of research (and cluster thinking) to be able to write a good query. Everything I have mentioned — about reading sample copies, analyzing the contents, getting an idea of the audience — all helps you to know and sell your market. You must make this very clear in your query. Note recent trends the magazine has been covering, comment on what will appeal to its readers — and by the way, when you're going through it, pay attention to the ads. They'll tell you a lot about the readership and the demographics: age, income, special interests, including sexual proclivities, background, education, and so on. A final caution: don't submit an idea on a subject that has recently been covered, nor do you submit a Christmas story in November. Remember that magazines, albeit swifter than books, still have a three-to-six-month lead time. Think Christmas in June. Timing counts. The same is true to some extent if you're hoping to cash in on a hot, current topic in the publishing field. You have to have the instincts of a carrion pigeon to get the lurid details of a sensational trial, disaster, or scandal into book form fast enough for a forgetful public to pay attention.

When I was writing my first queries, I had no previous publications to cite, so I simply ended on a positive, businesslike note, asking for the details of the assignment I expected: deadline? word count? When you don't have a steak to show, sell the sizzle.

Be sure to include a self-addressed, stamped envelope (SASE) with your query. In the case of American submissions, make a point of buying U.S. stamps next time you're in the States, or get a friend to mail you some. As for writing on spec, don't waste your time and effort on anything above nine hundred words, the length of an end-of-book column in a magazine, or a freelance slot in a newspaper. It's not a bad idea to try to break in on the short stuff, these small features, and work your way up to an assignment. This way you can let the editor know how reliable you are, not to mention entertaining, informative, prompt, and neat. Also prolific.

In the case of a short spec submission, instead of enclosing an SASE large enough and with enough postage to return the entire manuscript, simply clip in a self-addressed, stamped postcard (SASPC) and indicate that the copy need not be returned. This saves postage and effort on the returner's part. Some offices require that you spell it out, that in the event of rejection the material can be consigned to the shredder.

I do the same with play submissions. Some theatres, like some magazines now, require agented copy and will not consider manuscripts on spec. Others invite queries with sample dialogue (about ten pages) and a synopsis. There are a few that still (theoretically) will look at an entire script, in which case, don't hold your breath. Again, use an SASPC so that it's not necessary for the manuscript to be returned, thus saving you a lot of postage. A tip: print a small note across the top of your return address (I have postcards made with the same letterhead as my business letters) so you will know where it came from. I learned this, like other things, the hard way. I'd get a postcard back with a comment, signed "Al" or something, and I wouldn't have a clue where it came from. So write CGW for *Chicken Gazetteers Weekly*, or PCT for Podunk Community Theatre, or whatever, and save yourself a puzzlement when you get a mysterious postcard back in the mail.

Often a magazine will ask for clippings or tear sheets — samples of material you have published elsewhere. It is not mere ego that will make you very careful to keep a copy of everything you've published, it's good business; you never know when you'll need it to help you make another sale. Never, never let the only copy of anything out of the house, not just your own manuscripts but also tear sheets from magazines or newspapers. You cannot count on getting anything back. Take the time and trouble to go to a photocopier and get backup sheets of stuff and get several while you're at it. (Paperless society, my foot.)

Most magazine and book publishers will also tell you whether or not they will accept multiple submissions, so easy these days if you have your copy on file in your computer and a good printer that will give you fresh scripts at a moment's notice.

Follow-Up

After an interval of silence, you are entitled to nag. If you haven't heard from a magazine within six weeks, drop a letter or postcard asking whether or not your submission was received, and saying if not, you'll send another copy. But tell them if they have, then "No rush, take your time, okay, but do let me know so I can try somewhere else."

This goes for book publishers and theatres, too, but give them a little more time. I hate to generalize, but I do find that Canadians are more lax about responding than Americans. I have begun to send copies of my cover letters with additional SASPCs if I haven't heard from them in six months. After three or four of these noodges, I get a little sharp and suggest that if they needed the stamps so badly, they should have let me know. One cute dramaturge wrote me back and said actually, he'd torn the stamp off and written his grandmother. I liked that, and he read my play, too.

I despaired of another director to whom I had sent letter after letter over a period of a few years begging for a response, finally asking for, if nothing else, a brochure of the theatre's prospective season. I finally met him at an opening-night party of a play he had directed, which I attended with an actor who was in his cast. When I was introduced to him, I gave him a stamp. He did a double take, remembered my name, had the grace to blush, and has since been at least more prompt in his replies to me. He still hasn't done a play of mine, though, and probably never will. Never mind, theatre directors do not go on forever. They do, however, play musical chairs, so it never pays to alienate one completely. Sometimes you can't help it.

Of course, in order to nag in a timely manner, you must keep track of what you submit. You can keep a large calendar and write the name of the piece you submitted on the date it was mailed, then record the response, if any, later on the date you received a letter, go-ahead, rejection, request for more information, whatever. Bear in mind that it may be another year, another calendar, by the time you get a reply. You might find it simpler and less depressing to keep an annual scribbler with a page for each play/book/article you have submitted: where, when, results, remuneration. Or run a report file in your computer and keep track of it that way. With your original letter ready to be copied and re-sent, there's no doubt that computers make it easier for you to be an efficient nag .

One question, in fact the most common one I am asked, arises in every new writer's mind: "What if someone steals my ideas?" Not to worry. Like babies, there's more where they came from. Ideas cannot be protected by copyright; your expression of them can be, that is, your words. The copyright laws differ in Canada and the United States, but they are designed to protect the creator — somewhat. You have to be vigilant. If you're worried about the safety of your material, here's a simple way to safeguard it. Send yourself a copy by registered mail, and when you receive it, don't open it. The date on the sealed package is your proof of date and evidence of ownership. Mark the outside so you'll remember what it is and file it away.

My experience with editors, publishers, producers, and so on, has proved to me that, by and large, they honour their sources. If an idea came to them from you first, they'll come back to you to do something with it. I've often had assignments several months after I submitted an idea because at an editorial meeting when it was decided to go ahead with a story, someone remembered who first suggested it. You might want to be more careful about dropping ideas in front of other writers.

When you do get a nod, be eager, be polite, be prompt, and make your finished product even better than you promised. This is not to put words in editors' heads; be careful to deliver what they expect, and it doesn't hurt to get a very clear idea of their expectations. Ask questions, confirm what you suspected about the audience, and make sure both of you understand what your assignment is about. Also, pay attention to the word count specified and adhere to it. I know some writers who deliberately write about 10 percent more than the required number of words to allow for editing and cutting. This practice can backfire; it's as well to know your editor before you play games like that. The whole idea of writing as a business is epitomized in the way you handle your queries and subsequent assignments. You are not a Sunday hobbyist. You are a serious, reliable, disciplined, resourceful person, intent on making a living as well as a name for yourself.

One more thing, something I have never seen in any advice to writers: when you hand in your finished copy, submit another idea. Why quit when you're on a winning streak?

Life Beyond Queries, and in Between

When you're between assignments, you have to keep working, and not only at filling the mails. Again, let me offer a few suggestions for action. Of course, you always have to keep abreast of what's going on in your particular field. You do this by:

- **Reading:** newspaper reports, magazines in the related field, newsletters, and so on.
- **Reading:** good books, good writing, ideas, poetry — "the best," as Matthew Arnold put it, "that has been thought and said in the world."

- **Talking:** or schmoozing, as they call it in the movie business: meeting people, going to conferences, parties, finding out what's going on in the subject areas or genres you specialize in.
- **Listening:** to music, theatre, radio, entertainment, lectures.
- **Joining:** the union or association of like-minded professionals in your field who inform each other through their newsletter and exchanges. If you're intent on the magazine market, the Periodical Writers Association of Canada (PWAC) is a must. You have to qualify to join a professional group; ask for an application form if you think you're ready.
- **Joining:** subject-related associations or groups it would pay you to belong to for up-to-date information in your field. I was, for example, a founding member of Community Contacts for the Widowed in Toronto (now defunct), and of Bereaved Families of Ontario, both for obvious reasons.
- **Writing:** letters. Send SASEs and ask for guidelines or contest rules or whatever is available from your chosen markets. Also sample copies of magazines. You have to know your target.
- **Writing:** more queries!

You'll find you pick up more ideas as you go along, keeping a constant eye out for what publishers, editors, producers, and all your potential customers are buying. As you keep on writing, of course, you will have more product to sell. If you can't sell a piece in one form, perhaps a change of medium will improve its chances. A play can become a TV movie or a short story. A novel could become a children's story. A successful article on a hot topic could be scaled down for a children's or a young adult market. You often see hit movies turned into quickie novels to cash in on their sales. A short story can become a radio play, and vice versa. A radio play could be turned into a movie. Remember *Saturday Night Fever*, the enormously successful movie (1977) starring John Travolta in his other life? It began as an article in *New York* magazine.

If you can afford it, buy the annual market books (see Appendices) and watch for new outlets and markets, as well as for changes of personnel. Note: most of the directories are available in public libraries but you can't mark them up, scribble ideas for submissions as they occur to you, or plug them with sticky notes. Better to own them. What I do, to save money, is buy them every other year and then fill in new information as I spot it: new names or addresses or the death of a publishing house, theatre, magazine — it happens all the time, and seems to be getting more frequent. Keeping track helps to keep your directories from becoming obsolete quite so fast. Lately, I have subscribed to writersmarket.com on-line with its regular market updates and space for keeping tabs on your submissions. If you are a full-time freelancer, this would probably pay for itself with your first sale and, of course, its cost earns you tax credit.

Here is how a market search works. Begin, as I say, with your own copy of the latest *Writer's Market* (hard copy or on-line, though the on-line issue is not as good). (The following instructions can be applied to a fiction or poetry market, a publishers' or a theatre directory.) Read through every entry and cross out the ones that mean nothing to you. Circle the possibilities and write down ideas in the side margins as you go along, marking those pages with sticky notes. Later, go back through and scan your notes, choosing the most likely ideas to follow up on. Then start your submissions, obeying the injunctions in your targets' descriptions.

That is, do not submit entire manuscripts if they want only an outline (book) or synopsis (play) and a sample chapter or ten pages of dialogue. Note the magazines and publishers that will not accept multiple submissions — but they had better offer prompt response in return for what amounts to an exclusive offering. If they don't mention a self-imposed deadline, impose one. Say that if you don't hear from them within six weeks, you will be submitting the material elsewhere. Note also the ones that will read only agented material. By all means write for guidelines if they're offered and don't forget the SASE.

Pay attention, while you're at it, to what is usually a separate section in all these directories: a list of the available grants, retreats, fellowships, contests, and competitions and their deadlines. Again, cross out the ones that are simply not applicable to you. Especially note, if you are looking at a foreign country's offerings, whether other nationalities are welcome to enter or apply. No sense wasting their time and your postage.[6]

Watch especially for changes in personnel: a theatre or a publisher or a magazine that rejected your work in the past may have a change of mind and direction with a new leader, so you might want to resubmit. Then again, when an editor or publisher who liked your work moves on, see if you can follow him or her. Watch, too, what theatres are producing, note what publishers prefer, read what the magazines are pushing, look for film producers who do the kind of thing you write — any or all of these, depending on your chosen genre.

The one thing writers tend to forget when they're so intent on one project, or one all-consuming idea, is that their clients want product, lots of it. More than that, they want long-term production. They're not buying one idea, they're buying a whole person, a future, someone who is going to keep on supplying them with publishable, producible, saleable material. You could be that person.

The story is famous of Canadian icon Pierre Berton in his salad days, who sold the same story eighteen times with different leads and slant, and, of course, different writing, but using the research again and again, thus making it pay dividends over and above his initial expenditure of money and energy, making the most of the initial research. (It pays to keep your files.) This story is not so old as to be useless to you now; I spoke to Pierre about it when I was working on this book and he said he's recycling everything these days. Keep this in mind before you let go of any rights to your material. (I'm thinking electronic here.) You may be able to keep on selling it.

---

6 Do remember that other countries are remarkably partisan about their own stamps. Letters or manuscripts will not be returned to you with your country's stamps on them. Although International Mail Coupons are recommended, most mail clerks don't seem to know what to do with them. I use them if absolutely necessary for England.

As you produce more, you will have a backlog of material which people may want to reprint or excerpt or cite and for which they will (should) pay a fee. This is why it is so important for you to negotiate your rights, including electronic. Also, never mind what some writers tell you, that they've sold everything they ever wrote, making you feel like a nerd. They neglect to tell you when. Sure they sold their stuff, but they don't tell you how long it took them, or what the time gap was between creation and publication. I have written (short) things on spec that didn't sell the first time out, but that with a new lead sold to another market than the one I initially had in mind. I have also had material revert to me, sold to a magazine that went belly-up, leaving me free to peddle it again. Some material I have written has been edited out of the books I wrote them for; I have sold bits of it as short takes (out-takes?) to newspapers and magazines, and have even reincorporated them in subsequent reincarnations of the book they didn't appear in at first. Some of my books have been remaindered and I have recovered the copyright, then sold them again to a different (like this one) or the same (short-sighted) publisher but revised, updated, refurbished, and saleable once more. This is why it pays to keep things on file. In your memos to yourself on the publishing history of your material, it would be a good idea to keep track of the rights sold. If in doubt, check the contract.

Breaking into theatre is too big a subject to deal with here; the rule is, as elsewhere, start small and work locally, that is, with a new script. Once you've had something professionally produced, you can take a chance on offering the script or synopsis to a distant theatre, along with the play's history of production, plus reviews and your resumé. Don't hold your breath. Transom sales don't happen very often in any writer's life but they do happen. (They've happened to me.) Try instead, or also, to get your foot in the door with someone you know. This is the reason you go to parties, conferences, book launches, awards presentations, and even readings by other people. It's called schmoozing and it works.

As for books, in the case of fiction you usually have to submit the completed manuscript on spec, mandatory if it's a first novel, although

I note now that some publishers suggest a few sample chapters and an outline. The bad news is that a lot of publishers have cut their readers and require agented material or several months (read: a year!) to get to it. Bear in mind that a smaller package is less daunting to the poor, overworked publishing staff who are short of time and develop short attention spans. You're more likely to get news sooner, even if it's bad news. Once you have a track record, you can vary your approach. However, it's a different story with non-fiction books.

You can often get a sale, or at least a nibble of interest, with the submission of two or three chapters, a comprehensive outline, and a dynamite pitch. By sale, I mean a contract engaging to buy your book with an advance against royalties to help pay for your time while you write it. That's how I got lured into writing non-fiction books: with money up front.

As noted, the best way to break into magazines is through the short stuff that can be written and submitted on spec: back-of-book comments, humorous features, commentary of some kind. Get your foot in the door, your byline on the pages, and begin a dialogue with a friendly editor. Be chatty, be friendly, sparkle with ideas and energy, and start getting paid. More magazines cram the newsstands than ever before but — or and, depending on your point of view — they specialize. Pick any field of interest, any area of expertise, and you'll find a magazine, often more than one, devoted to it. If you happen to be an expert on butterflies, you may have a whole new career fluttering ahead of you.

In the great heyday of general magazines, fiction drew a lot of readers and supported many well-known writers. Sadly, fiction and attention spans have dwindled over the years. Now you have to search for magazines that buy it regularly; when they do, they want fewer words and more punch for less money. I have a nonagenarian friend, Hope Davis, who used to write for the great women's magazines, like *Ladies' Home Journal, Women's Home Companion,* and *Good Housekeeping,* in the thirties, forties, and fifties. In those days a magazine writer, and that meant a fiction writer, could make a good living on six to twelve stories a year, renting an apartment in New York and having fun. A magazine paid $1,000 to $2,500 for a short story (three to four thousand words) and the living was easy. Today, fiction stories, but shorter and fewer of them, still pay $1,000 to $2,500, though less often. In the meantime, the price of apartments in New York has gone way up.

If you are intent on fiction and can afford it, you will have to build and subsidize your own track record with publication in the literary magazines, which not only don't pay, they now also charge entry fees for the contests they stage regularly as fundraisers. I often think that their only readers must be other writers who bought a subscription with their entry fee.

INCOME

About a year before I moved to my lake retreat, I was commissioned by the *United Church Observer* to write a piece, with an apology for the low rate — $750. Ten years later, the *Observer* came back to me with a request for another piece and they were still paying the same fee (plus GST for the government, an increase in their expense but not in my income), with no apologies. I wrote the piece but commented, when I sent it in, that I found it sad that they had not raised their fees to writers since I was certain that during that same period of time their rent, heat, light, and phone expenses had gone up, as no doubt had the salaries of their cleaning staff.

I moved into Toronto (from Stratford) in 1975 to pursue a career as a writer, or maybe not a career — a living. I made my way initially in journalism: magazine and newspaper work. With other downtrodden journalists I attended a few impassioned meetings and became a founding member in 1976 of PWAC. One of the new organization's first efforts was to convince the magazines that they should raise writers' fees, unchanged for the previous twenty-some years. They succeeded, but got stuck there; fees have remained largely unchanged since then.

In April 1997, PWAC announced the results of a new survey revealing that annual incomes for freelance writers had remained on hold for eighteen years. Lower by 11 percent than the average Canadian worker's salary, freelance writers' incomes since 1979 have risen by about $463, not enough to meet the rising cost of living. This, in spite of the fact that the average PWAC member holds two post-secondary degrees and has worked as a freelance writer for ten years. That tells you something about the respect accorded to writers.

Newspapers generally pay less than magazines and have tended to use their staff writers; most have offered a few venues for outside talent, usually book reviews. Both are at risk now, trying to navigate the information highway without a crossing guard. What we all have to beware of now is becoming roadkill. We'll get to that. Right now, the freelance market is not as attractive as it used to be because of the danger to writers of getting run over.

Besides providing a small injection of money, short stuff offers you some exposure and publicity; you always get to give a scintilla of information about yourself with your identifying byline, as, for example, "Janice Trueblood's latest novel is *Granny, We Hardly Knew You,*" or if you have no recent publication, you can say "JT specializes in ghost stories," or whatever.

Have you considered a column? Not the fabled tap-dancing of a well-known columnist, to be sure, but a more modest effort, at least to begin with. Small, low-paying magazines and weeklies might be willing to pay you something on a regular basis for seven to nine hundred words about a topic dear to their readers' hearts. I myself have been offered ten cents a word for a column (ceiling $75) in a quarterly up where I live.

Seniors, by the way, get a lot of ink these days. Check your *Writer's Market* and your *Canadian Writer's Market* and take a look at how many magazines are specifically directed at the interests of elders. Your age need have nothing to do with what you write as long as there are no liver spots on the paper. Twenty years ago I used to have a monthly column in *Miss*

Chatelaine magazine — now *Flare* — and I was forty-something then, advising young women on their "Habits" (the name of the column).

The tempting prospect of a column is that it could become a hit and you could be syndicated. Look at Erma Bombeck. She started for peanuts and parlayed them into diamonds and worldwide fame. You may not want to be another Molly Ivins or P.J. O'Rourke or Dave Barry or Sondra Gotlieb or Joey Slinger, but a small column that pays for your cornflakes wouldn't hurt.

Included in this analysis of possible sources of income, don't overlook revenue from sources other than commercial publications. If you have published a book, you will be delighted to receive one of the nicest bonuses going: the Public Lending Right (PLR) payment. After thirteen years of lobbying, TWUC persuaded the Canadian government to join eleven other countries in the world to pay authors for the presence in the country's libraries of copies of their books.[7] Whether or not you are a Union member, if you have a published book and are registered with PLR, you reap this little harvest every year, sometimes dwindling but maintaining over the last few years. The amount of money has to be replenished as more and more writers and books are involved. As it stands now, the ISBNs of your books are registered with PLR, with any new publications added each year (your responsibility) and as long as they are not how-to books, like this one, you will receive some money.

Then there are honoraria, fees, royalties, readings, workshops, seminars, and TV appearances. A word about that last: most television stations think you should be grateful to be up there in TV-land without demanding to be paid. Most of the time you are, and so are your publishers, when you're getting free publicity for your latest book. Never mind that the station is getting its content free, you must be affable, affable, affable. This is all part of book promotion. But when a channel calls you and wants you to be the expert on some program where they

---

7 A basic sum is paid for each title found in a random selection of ten libraries, with a ceiling that depends on the overall amount of money available. You get it in the multiplication, and it's better than the total royalty on ten copies.

want to do an "in-depth study" or a human-interest story, then listen to them try to wriggle out of paying you. Tell them you're a member of ACTRA (assuming you joined as soon as you became eligible; there's a point system which is explained to you on the application form). Repeat the rules they already know: that you can waive your fee and perform for nothing if you are promoting a book, but that if they want your expertise for their own purposes, you have to be paid. Even if you do get paid, it will seldom be even equity scale; you will receive an "honorarium" — about $150 — if you're lucky. Ask for expenses as well: parking, and, in my case, gas, add up. Save your receipts and submit them, but keep copies because you may have to nag. You could always say no.

Now we come to grants, fellowships, awards, retreats, and so on, the modern version of patronage. These are the goodies you apply for. We could never go back to patronage now; too many people are literate and there aren't many affluent kings or cardinals around. Of course, the big bucks and honours come from the prestigious prizes and I won't begin to go into the politics of those. We're talking survival here. Surely it's not too much to ask for a grant to enable you to subsist (not exist, not live) for a few months to a year in order to focus on a project dear to your heart and soul and perhaps even valuable to your country. Well, it is, because six times as many people apply as there are grants. This is what you are told when you receive your rejection. Not enough money to go around. Still, there are ways. Let me count the ways.

First, you have to know what's available, and I quote from the latest Canada Council update. (Note: the new guidelines will be published about the same time as this book, so be sure to check if you plan to apply.)

Grants for Professional Writers

The objective of the Grants for Professional Writers program is to encourage the development of Canadian writers — whether emerging, mid-career, or established. The program provides four types of support: Creative

Writing Grants, Senior Fellowships, Travel Grants and Author Residencies.

- Creative Writing Grants provide support to authors working on new projects in the fields of novel, short story, poetry, children's literature, graphic novel and literary non-fiction. Literature creation projects based on spoken word or the use of electronic technology and in which literary creation plays a key role may be submitted to the Spoken and Electronic Words Program of the Writing and Publishing Section. Playwrights who require funding to write a play should contact the Canada Council Theatre Section. Screen writers who require funding to write a screen play should contact the Media Arts Section.
- Senior Fellowships are given to established writers to enable them to cover costs related to a research and writing project in recognition of their professional achievements. The objective of this component is to make it possible for writers to lengthen the duration of their research and writing project.
- Travel Grants enable writers and translators to respond to invitations on occasions that are of great importance to their career. To attend the launching of their books by a foreign publisher, writers should henceforth contact the Outreach Office. A Canadian translator may also apply to this program to attend the launching of a book abroad for which he/she has provided the translation, if accompanied by the author.
- Author Residencies provide financial assistance to organizations such as post-secondary institutions, public libraries or writers' associations that wish to retain the services of a writer-in-residence and are

able to match the contribution made by the Canada Council for the Arts. The purpose of the residency is to encourage exchanges between the author and the community, and to enable the author to work on a writing project.

Applicants must be Canadian citizens or permanent residents of Canada. They must be recognized professional writers who have had:

- at least one book published by a professional publishing house; or
- a minimum of four texts of creative writing (e.g. short stories, excerpts from a novel) published on two separate occasions in literary magazines, recognized periodicals (including certain electronic periodicals and consumer magazines) or anthologies published by professional publishing houses. For poetry, a minimum of 10 published poems is required; or
- a minimum of 40 pages (10,000 words) of articles published in literary magazines, recognized periodicals or anthologies published by professional publishing houses.

The Canada Council accepts writing projects in all languages. Literary artists working in oral traditions are also eligible. They must be recognized as professionals by their peers (artists who work in the same artistic tradition), have specialized training in the field (not necessarily in academic institutions) and have been paid for their work.

Collaborative projects are accepted in this program, and writers may collaborate with professional artists from disciplines other than writing. One single artist makes the application, but full-time students are not eligible to apply.

Applicants may only apply for one Grant to Professional Artists per fiscal year (between 1 April and 31 March). Individual artists may receive up to two Grants to Professional Artists from the Canada Council in any 48-month period. Artists may also submit one request for a Travel Grant per year. Applicants must have submitted a final report on the use of any previous Canada Council grant to be eligible to apply to this program.

Write, phone, or fax for an application form, together with an Information Sheet. Do not send applications by fax or e-mail. Read the guidelines before calling the Council with questions. The relevant address and numbers are in the Appendix.

The application form is in the nature of a scavenger hunt list, deserving close attention, considering the prize. Once you've gone to the effort of compiling an application with your careful description of your project, your battery of references, and all the accompanying sample material, send it somewhere else after you've been rejected, either back to CanCow as soon as you're allowed (you have to wait out a turn) or — on a different application form, of course — to some other cash cow (granting body).

With a CanCow application you don't get to see your reference because you must send your referee (with prior consent requested and granted) a form to pass on directly. However, the Council will keep such material on file for a limited time. Unless one of your referees dies, you can keep on using his/her reference for a few years without going back to source or trying for a new affidavit because you haven't changed that much (improved, maybe).

Some grant applications require several references to be copied and sent in accompanying your other material. In this case, make a point of keeping copies, to be used again while the dates are still valid.

If you cross genres in your work, you may be in luck because it gives you different fields to apply in, in my case, theatre and writing, and now there are, as mentioned, some writer-in-library or -in-residence incumbencies available, as well as some decent non-fiction (*belles lettres*) grants. Thank writers like Pierre Berton and June Callwood who were instrumental in preventing a two-tier system of membership or opportunity in the Writers' Union and among reading and grant programs; because of them, non-fiction is recognized as a category. You can't be too academic and you also can't be practical, as in how-to or cookbooks. Humour isn't serious, history is honourable, *belles lettres* are okay.

Don't think you can awe your jury[8] with your references. I've noticed and had it concurred by others that, depending on their age and background, most of them have never heard of the impressive champions you have assembled. Shill was the late W.O. Mitchell's term for writing a glowing reference for a protegé. I hope your reference is glowing. I've heard of some recommenders who damned their applicant with such faint praise as to wipe out all hope of consideration. Not that you can ever see what is said. As I mentioned, you have to send a form to your references, along with a description of your project, and hope that they send something in on time. A word of advice: be sure to enclose with the form you send to your recommenders a stamped, addressed envelope, thereby saving the angels effort and postage — a small courtesy. And don't forget to write a thank-you letter, whether or not you get the grant.

Anyway, don't be too sure that the jury ever heard of your recommenders. You have to be political here, and I'm not sure how I can advise you. Choose, of course, someone who knows you, someone in your field who knows your work; choose representation of both genders; choose, if you are well acquainted, a member of a visible minority, because although everyone is bending over backward now to affirm equal rights, some rights are more equal than others. People don't really change, just the current attitudes.

If all else fails, try to get on a jury yourself, though that can be difficult. That way you'll earn a little money and view the politics first-

---

8   A Canada Council jury comprises three writers in your genre who receive a small fee for reading and passing judgment on their peers. They are usually chosen for the fact that they have run the gauntlet themselves in times past and actually won a grant.

hand. Usually, to get on a jury, you have to be a previous grant recipient yourself. Catch-22.

Choose your shill carefully with an eye to your potential judges' knowledge. When I applied to The MacDowell Colony (a prestigious artists' retreat in New Hampshire), one of my references was the actor Hume Cronyn. He told me he had been too busy to write a letter so he picked up the phone and said, "You have to accept that woman!" That got me in.

It's more than likely that you will not succeed in winning a grant the first or second or even third time out. Keep trying. As long as your references are still valid, it doesn't take much effort to apply after the first time; you get used to it. Do keep this in mind: your chances of getting a grant decrease even more if you don't apply.

Fellowships and retreats and writers-in-residencies are other ways of covering your living expenses for a specified period and must be handled in the same way, with an array of references and support material, which takes some time and some expense to assemble. If you win a slot in a retreat or are granted a fellowship or residency, the rewards are mixed. Certainly, at most retreats you get your room and board, if not entirely, then mightily, subsidized. If the snow falls, you don't have to shovel it; the food is good and you don't have to cook it; there's always someone to talk to, other like-minded souls to share your anger and inspiration, and to waste too much of your time, if you're not careful.

Writers-in-residence programs are tough wherever you find them. For a fixed, modest salary you must live in the city (accommodation at your own expense) where the residency is offered and perform several different duties: one or two public seminars are expected, performed by you, plus several readings, arranged by you, in addition to a usually weekly workshop with a nucleus of hopeful writers, plus one-on-one consultations with writers whose submitted manuscripts will keep you busy reading and editing in your spare time. If you are terribly conscientious, you will have little time for yourself; nevertheless, a lot of writers manage to complete a manuscript of their own while in residence.

At least you will have a steady income for a few months (up to a year), an office, and access to a library whose quality depends on the prestige and finances of the host.

For long-term freelancers it's a heady experience to enjoy a regular salary, even for a short time. The knowledge that there is a paycheque coming every other week is reassuring. Bills are paid on time, life seems secure. It's enough to make you contemplate getting a job, but then you'd have to give up your freedom!

Like other programs, the writer-in-library residencies have dwindled, but some large libraries, including university ones, still offer them. The stipend usually runs from $15,000 to a high of $25,000 for a ten-month term with few or no perks regarding living expenses or transportation. You have to be very portable and leave no expenses behind you, such as a lease or mortgage, or else get a reliable tenant to cover them while you're gone. It's easier for a single or a childless writer, preferably one with few possessions, to be this movable. Household goods cost a lot to ship and books are heavy.

So these are the various sources of income for an enterprising free-lancer. You've assessed your skill, your subjects, your markets, and your possibilities. Now you have to assess your personal situation: your age, health, and energy; marital status and dependants, if any; your support system and immediate prospects; your savings, your expenses, and your projected income over the next year — two, if possible. If you are young and healthy and single with no dependants, you can afford to gamble on yourself and take a few risks. It's even kind of fun to live in a garret — for a while. By the time they're thirty-five, most actors and writers I have known get tired of a mattress on the floor and tuna fish for supper, no decent clothes, and never enough money for the books they would love to own or the performances they would like to attend, and wish they had some real furniture. So they settle for a regular job with a regular paycheque, not that there's that much guarantee in jobs these days. You might as well keep on keeping on. Do you have a cheap source of paper?

The rule, even for people with jobs, is that you should have the equivalent of three months' (six months' is better) salary in liquid form in case of emergency. Emergency means losing your day job, which you are about to. Liquid means accessible. It used to mean in a savings account, but even premium savings accounts in banks pay precious little these days. Take a look, at least, at term deposits which yield slightly more interest according to the length of the term; GICs, also low, but with a slightly higher yield if you can afford to lock them in for a longer period; and T-bills, short-term quick turnover in case you need fast cash. That's your cushion, if you can manage one.

Do you have any income at all? Some young writers are lucky enough to be granted a stake from their parents or an indulgent aunt, usually with a time limit, but it's something. Patronage isn't what it used to be in the days of Mozart and Leonardo da Vinci, and the kind of government patronage we're getting these days resembles a lottery more than a statement of faith in the future of culture.

Some freelancers can wangle pay for special part-time services that give them a base to live on. I met a visual artist, a whiz with figures, who does the books for several of her friends who pay her. An actor friend of mine acts as a housekeeper in the old sense of the word and personal secretary to a rich woman who lives in a mansion and lets my friend take a leave of absence when she gets a part in a play. I know more than a couple of writers and one director with excellent secretarial skills who have worked as temps when times were tough. I am not recommending part-time jobs out of your field, but they are there, though scarcer than they were. Of course, some writers are spouses, both male and female. It usually costs a writing wife more time at the home job because she hasn't developed a lower level of tolerance for dirt and clutter. I can name several male writers whose wives, not writers, make much more money than they do, and who have worked out a more equitable arrangement than writing wives have with their husbands. Some writers have become househusbands and learned to cook quite well, but none of them, to my knowledge, has ever cleaned a toilet. When one of these men became a father, he added nanny service to his home help, thus forcing him to rent an office and work at his writing at night. He's divorced now.

A Saving Grace

Any way you look at it, as a freelancer you're going to have to hustle. While cutting costs on the one hand, and living as economically as possible, you must also keep trying to increase your income with the other (preferably both hands). What I'm going to tell you now may seem intrusive when you're trying so hard to make ends meet, but I must recommend that you save 10 percent of your income, however meager it is. This may seem too hard to do when you receive $200 for a book review, plus $14 GST that you're going to have to give to the government (as soon as your income reaches $30,000 annually and you acquire a GST number) — not only hard but impossible to take $20 out and stick it somewhere else. It is hard. You'll find it easier, in fact, relatively painless, if you simply estimate your income annually or every six months if it's too bleak, and arrange for 10 percent of it to be automatically removed from your chequing account every month. You can have this money withdrawn and paid into a Canada Savings Bond or an RRSP account or into mutual funds. With dollar cost averaging and accrued dividends, even a small investment, like $50 a month, can begin to add up, the sooner the better. I hope 10 percent of your income adds up to more than that.

Be warned: mutual funds are not as liquid, that is, readily cashable, as other savings vehicles because there's usually a withdrawal charge within the first five years. However, within the funds family you join, it is possible to move your funds around for no charge following winning streaks, not as slavishly as the stock market, but often enough to take advantage of good investments on the part of the fund managers.

As for insurance, disability is far more important than life insurance at this point. If you have dependants, by all means set up some sort of safety net for them; term insurance is cheaper. But a fate worse than death awaits if you become too disabled to write. I broached this to my insurance agent when I was starting out and he scoffed, saying I could still write with a broken leg, but he was wrong. It's not that easy to write when you are in physical pain. I found that out when I was suffering a chronic backache for over a year during which I could barely sit down. I tried to write with a pen, standing up, with a couple of telephone books on a table to raise the height of my paper, but it wasn't very satisfactory and I wasn't thinking too clearly with all the painkillers I was taking. By that time I actually had disability insurance. One of the reasons I joined TWUC was that Mutual Life of Omaha had made group disability insurance available to members. I applied for some assistance but was turned down; the fine print in the policy defined eligibility for a payout so craftily that the company didn't have to pay me. All I can say is: yes, get disability insurance, but be careful. Read the fine print. Fortunately, I got better and cranked up the earning machine again.

You will, in addition to spending less and saving some, while earning as much money as you can, have to keep a careful tally of your expenses for income tax purposes. While you don't get any company benefits or insurance or bonuses or a private pension plan,[9] nevertheless as a freelance, self-employed writer you do get a number of tax breaks in terms of your deductible claims, now called tax credits. Once you have some income to show for your pains, which proves that you are indeed a practising, professional writer, then you can begin to show what it costs you to earn that money. The funny, true thing is that almost everything you do is caused by or aimed at your work. Save all your receipts. My idea of a complete holiday would be to go somewhere and not ask for a receipt. It doesn't happen. Everything I do has an ulterior motive and a justifiable rationalization.

---

9 Your Canada Pension Plan payments are deducted automatically when you file your income tax return.

I am an extremely, painfully honest person. I always tell a cashier when she has made an error in my favour; I always give back an overage in change. I do fudge a little on my customs declarations but only to the extent of rounding off figures to the lower, not the higher, nearest zero. I certainly do not evade my income tax, though I wish the government would spend my money more wisely. However, I do avoid paying more than I have to.

The Canadian Goods and Services Tax (GST) is a real pain to calculate quarterly as, like any small businessperson, you and I must do, but I choose not to take the shortcut because by income tax time most of the paperwork is done and it takes less time to prepare reports for an accountant. You may be a whiz who won't need to spend your money on such professional help. I'm not and I do. Never have I attempted to estimate my own taxes. Every year my accountant tells me he loves me dearly and he wouldn't touch my account were it not for this fact, because it's one of the worst he does. Not because I make a lot of money, because I don't, but because I make money from so many different sources and I have so many disparate expenses that it's a hassle to calculate. If you are a busy freelancer you will have the same problem.

I make reading fees and script fees and box office percentages, royalties and advances against royalties, and honoraria, grants, and stipends, as well as dividends — but no bonuses. I pay agents' fees and ACTRA and WGC (Writers' Guild of Canada) fees and various union dues and memberships in professional organizations. I have enormous research costs and I buy tons of paper supplies (and write on the blank underside of every page I lay my hands on). Years ago now I was investigated by the revenue people because someone reported that I seemed to be awfully busy, popping up in print everywhere. The conclusion of the man who came to look at my books was that I was honest to a fault and not very smart. So now I have an accountant. He is not the only expert I rely on. You will find, as I did, that you do need helping hands — and brains are even better.

Sooner or later you are going to ask yourself if you need to be incorporated. Ask your accountant. It may sound impressive and businesslike to be so, but it costs a lot to set it up, and until you're making an indecent amount of money or spasmodic lumps of it that must be parcelled out judiciously, it won't do you much good.

OFFICE EQUIPMENT

I hope I've made it clear by now that you are a writing machine, or should be. You've programmed yourself, you have the material and the markets. You're selling. To keep functioning you have to have everything smoothly running, serving your needs without a hitch. This includes your physical space, equipment, tools, and supplies, as well as your physical state and the arrangements you've made for both.

If you are serious about your writing you have to have serious space. The corner of the kitchen table won't do, although I do know one writer, a novelist, who gets up early every day, makes a pot of coffee, and writes longhand at his kitchen table (for four hours). He owns the whole house, though, with a real office in it, and there are no children dropping Pop Tart crumbs all over his manuscript. You might be happier with an office.

I know other writers who have rented a room away from home to give them privacy, silence (in a city environment?), and freedom to litter as they please, that is, to leave the accumulating piles of paper untouched until a project is completed. This solution is more expensive than it used to be and most writers have gone home again. (Rich ones have a studio at the bottom of the garden and a serf/spouse who brings them lunch.) There is a growing tendency now to work at home, and not only among writers, but writers can move further away, as I did when I settled in a (winterized) cottage on a lake north of Toronto. Sometimes this move out of a city can save money, but watch it. I found that what I saved on makeup and panty hose, impulsive lunches out and nights at the theatre, I spent on hydro. And I had to put supports under the floor to bear the weight of all my paper and books.

Whether you write with a typewriter, word processor (glorified typewriter), office computer, or laptop, you must pay attention to your physical setup, not the space but the desk and chair and the relationship between you and your machine. I read that the late Barbara Cartland wrote on a chaise longue, dictating her romantic stories while eating chocolates. She specialized in soft centres. Truman Capote was supposed to have written lying down with a portable typewriter on his chest. What do you do? Pay attention, before you end up in pain.

By this time you have probably accumulated daunting numbers of files: seed beds, free-fall writing, ideas, plus works-in-progress, published pieces, and of course books, your own and others'. You have tear sheets, reviews, and interviews, and you also have clippings of news items or things that appealed to you that you think you might use someday — not quite seed beds but not quite trash, either.

What do you do with them?

Years ago I used to think happiness lay in owning one file cabinet, preferable to the cardboard Carnation tinned-milk carton I used to store my file folders. Now, with five file cabinets and countless cardboard file boxes, I know that such happiness is elusive and the real answer lies in my (spasmodic) attempts to quell the rising tide of paper. Just recently I found a wonderful way to solve the problem.

I gave away all my files, my memories, my regrets, frustrations, triumphs, disappointments, defeats, posters, mementos, three acorns, and a dead mouse. I packed them in twenty-eight boxes and shipped them collect to the Archives of the University of Manitoba. For this I was given a large tax credit, larger than my minuscule income really needed, but it was nice. For a while my joke was that truly, tomorrow was the first day of the rest of my life, and it felt very good. But then the tide turned, and I have more filing to do.

If you reach my Grey Eminence, you, too, could send your paper detritus to a place with more shelves than you have. In the meantime, you should probably study one of those organizational books that promise more time and energy and space if you follow their suggestions. It helps, for a while. Everything does, for a while.

I will say this, by way of comfort: one of the nicest things about not filing is finding obsolete material when you finally get around to it, papers that you can throw away with impunity and a gladsome heart. You might consider this neglect as a first-line filing system, giving the material time to ripen, age, grow valuable or useless as the case may be before you decide what to do with it.

Here are a few things you can do to try to slow the flow:

- Have more than one filing system. This sounds ridiculous but it helps me to keep very handy a few current folders for clippings and ideas about something that is incubating. The same is true for something you're working on that will eventually go into a historical file but that needs to be *au courant* for the moment.
- Handle each piece of paper only once. This is nonsense but it's what efficiency experts tell you to do. Whether or not I do this depends on what else I'm doing. If I'm working on something major, the mail, for example, gets glanced at and either thrown out or piled up for later attention.
- Please, tell me how to keep ahead of all my newspaper clippings. Some are easy to file, if they're about current projects. Others are small enough to go into seed beds. Others get dumped into a file-later pile. The nicest thing about the delay, as I say, is that when I do finally get around to it, a lot of the stuff is obsolete or irrelevant. If it's still valid, then it deserves to be saved. Just be sure you noted the publication, source, writer, and pub date or the item will be useless.
- One more thing: if you have been slow to file odd clippings and newsy items, you will usually discover when you return to them a certain pattern, a recurring theme. Suddenly, instead of a generic interest, you find you have a specific angle. Now you have a sepa-

rate file folder, or box, or seed-bed, book, or pile. Your next seed has germinated.

Of course, besides the space and the filing system, you need the tools, your physical aids like paper, pen, typewriter or computer, stylus, palimpsest. (A computer disk is very like a palimpsest in that it can be erased but retains impressions. Eerie.) You also need some basic references: a dictionary, thesaurus, and an encyclopedia would be nice. (Note: all of these are available in CD-ROM now, swift to access and compact to store.) Other material will depend on your areas of specialty. It all adds up.

VIGNETTE

There's an apocryphal story about Dorothy Parker during the early days of *The New Yorker* magazine. She met the editor, Harold Ross, on the street one day and he asked her why she hadn't come in to write a story for him. Her explanation was simple: "Someone was using the pencil."

These days it costs more than a pencil to be a writer, even if you're a member of the Lead Pencil Club. Publishers want not only hard copy but also disks, and guess who pays for them? In the effort to get your copy to them yesterday, you have to pay e-mail or fax or courier costs. If you live in the same city as the book or magazine publisher, I recommend that you hand-deliver the material, as I used to do, and still try to do, when I can. It not only saves time, it also guarantees safe arrival. I can tell you horror stories, which I'm sure you can match, about late, deflected, and lost shipments even when sent by courier or Xpresspost, which must have gone out by pony express and been trapped in a blizzard on a mountain pass.

You would be wise to do some bulk buying of your most necessary supplies because, although it involves an initial outlay of capital, you will save money in the long run. Several office-supply stores offer discount bargains, while others grant a discount to members, for example, of PWAC. Years ago, when the first computer frenzy swept the writers of Canada, a special sale through TWUC turned most writers into IBM clones. While we're onto electronic supplies, I'm sure you've already considered or bought a laser printer. If you live, as I do, outside of a city, it pays to own one. Where I live, the nearest copier (forty-five kilometres away) does one sheet at a time, without collating, and costs thirty-five cents per page. Once I have a script on file, or stored in a backup disk, I can call it up and print out any number of perfect copies without having to leave the house. I have my own electric three-hole punch (bought at a year-end sale) and a selection of covers, folders, binders (also purchased at a discount), and so on, to package them. The only thing I can't get a bargain on is postage.

Book Promotion

You may wonder why I include such a seemingly narrow consideration as the promotion of books in a generic book for freelance writers. The reason lies in the poor financial returns in the periodical industry. The frozen fee structure has forced seasoned writers out of the field in search of other, more lucrative sources of income. These have included business, corporate and speech writing, ghostwriting, maybe some screen or television writing, and a book or more of one's own, although with the hole the publishers keep digging themselves into, one wonders how long that will remain a viable option. Midlists are disappearing in both Canada and the United States, books by respectable writers with a modest but solid track record. The publishers give those fabled advances to the really big names and cut back on the print runs for all but the blockbusters. By the time a journalist has hit middle age, still hustling just as hard for less money, a book seems like a good idea. At least, it will give you some credibility and look good on your resumé. Anyway, here you are: for some reason that escapes you now, you find you have written a book and it's going to be published. Now what?

As someone who prefers to spend time alone in the company of one's thoughts, I found the prospect of going out to hustle not all that attractive. This kind of split happens, I think, to every writer: you begin as a quiet introvert, but there are times when you must become a wild extrovert. A little ego goes a long way and seldom carries one as far as an eager publicist seems to want to take one (if he or she is any good). On the other hand, be grateful for an eager publicist; it means your publishers think you are worth peddling.

Yes, yes, you agree to let them use your name, likeness, photograph, whatever, in connection with pushing your book and you hope they will promote it. You also agree to make yourself available and give reasonable assistance in the promotion of the Work. You want all the publicity you can get. The fact is, you have to have a saleable product, something interviewers and, ultimately, readers are interested in. Of course, it helps if your book is topical, and a bonus if it's well written.

Book writers enjoy complaining about tours and I'm not sure they don't have a point. You want to get the public's attention, but a spring or fall migration is not necessarily the best way to do it. An excerpt in a newspaper or magazine might catch more readers; a television or radio adaptation or — best — a movie based on it does wonders for sales. That takes time and luck and hustle, but it happens. Blurbs help, that is, endorsements by famous people who like your work. Look at what Oprah Winfrey did for the writers of her favourite books: miraculous sales, heaving writers onto the best-seller lists, some of them even belated and from relative obscurity. Exposure is the key, but it has to be the kind of exposure that whets the desire to buy your book.

Once your book is published, you have about a six-week window to sell it before it is shoved off the shelves by the next lot, unless you happen to have hit some section of the book-buying public right between the eyes. After that, it's up to you to try to keep your book in view. I used to be shy, but no longer am, about looking for my book(s) on the bottom shelf, because I'm a *W*, and lifting them up to eye level so they can be seen — and purchased. I also (unless I am feeling incredibly shy or haven't washed my hair) introduce myself to the sales clerks and offer to sign any books in stock. After I get home I nag my publishers about keeping their backlists in the bookstores. The publishers say it's the booksellers' fault if your books aren't there; the sellers blame the publishers. Here's a parable about books in terms of a popular grocery item.

PARABLE

Once upon a time a woman went into her little local grocery store and looked for Clamato juice: none in stock. She urged the grocer to get some, assuring him others would buy it as well. So the grocer brought in a case of Clamato juice and for a while the woman was happy to have it available when she wanted it. But one day when she went to buy another bottle of Clamato juice, it was all gone. She waited a week for new stock to come in but there was still no Clamato juice. Finally, she asked the grocer about it.

"Why don't you get some more Clamato juice?" she asked.

"Well, you know," the grocer said, "I couldn't keep it on the shelf."

That's how booksellers appear to treat books. They sell their order and then they have the next books on the lists to think about. Books are like cottage cheese to them and they have to make room for the new batch. Backlists, of course, are another story. Both publishers' reps and booksellers should be aware of the perennial favourites that go on and on and that should be available.

You will always be your own work's best salesperson. If you're too shy and retiring and introspective to change, then don't. (And quit writing.) But if you agree to be a hustler, then be a confident, aggressive one. Also a nag, a thorn in the side of your publisher, and a cheerful and tenacious guest on any TV or radio show that will have you. In addition, you are going to have to think up different angles, scams, and tie-ins in order to get more ink, more exposure, more coverage for you and your child.

Publishing is not the only field where you have to cooperate and help to sell your product. Much the same routine applies to play promotion. Again, you'll find yourself on the interview circuit, but you have an advantage sometimes, if your actors are willing to talk — or act — for you. Again, though, any hooks or tie-ins you can think of might help. I saved an article from *American Theatre* magazine by a playwright describing his publicity efforts on behalf of a small, off-off-Broadway production. He used postcards to friends and critics; he sent copies of reviews and wooed other reviewers; he stuck posters in local restaurants, distributed flyers in hairdressing salons and wine stores; in short, he hustled, right down to the last night his play was on. That's what it takes. A theatre in Boston asked to produce his play, so it paid off.

There's a lot you can do. Even after the book has launched, you can continue to offer some help. From the time I first started travelling with my work, I have let the promotion people know where and when I was going somewhere so they could go piggyback on my trips, that is, take advantage of my presence in another city at very little cost to themselves. You can do this. If it's possible for you to stay over with a friend in order to go on a show, do it, but sometimes your publishers will be willing to pay for a hotel bed for one night to keep you in place. Beds don't cost as much as planes. Be prepared to be humble, though. The publisher does have to pay a rep in the city you're in to set up even a couple of interviews and they might not think you're worth it. As I say, humble.

After a while, though, when you've had a few books published and have been around the circuit a few times, you might have developed one or two contacts of your own in other cities, people who seemed to enjoy talking to you and who might be interested in another chat. Let them know when you'll be in their city and see if you can arrange something.

Same idea with the bookstores. You've signed books for them before; go in and see if your books are in stock, offer to sign them, and if you have an appropriate subject and enough time, offer a reading or a talk or a workshop or a Q & A session.

Non-fiction books are easier to promote because interviewers don't have to read them. They can handle them simply by looking at the blurb on the cover and talking about content and guessing a lot, and you can (gently) correct them when they get it wrong. No one ever talks about a writer's writing, not when it's non-fiction. Non-fiction writers merely report about things, and things are easier for most interviewers to get a handle on; they can be dealt with in a five-minute bite. The host's job is tough enough. How would you like to have to read three or four books a night and sound intelligent about them the next day — for the entire season of migratory writers? You can help the interview along with a few hints or well-placed questions. Make your hosts look good so you'll look good and be invited back.

Here's a little list of things you can do to help keep your book on the shelves and off the remainder lists — for a while, anyway. Maybe you'll even sell a few copies.

- Ask the publisher to print a little postcard with a blurb about your book and use it instead of stationery for all your letters (I did this with one of my cookbooks, sending a recipe). Your postage, by the way, is a very legitimate expense. I do this for my plays, too, photocopying something from the program.
- Drop a friendly note to any book reviewers or magazine editors you know personally, just to remind them you and your book exist.
- Write something around the subject (remembering what you are not allowed to use according to your contract) for a cash crop sale to a guest column in a newspaper. If your subject doesn't lend itself to a brief, amusing summary, write about something you learned while writing your book or play, or

about people's reactions to you because they didn't know you knew so much about stars, or sex, or poison, or whatever.

- By all means write a feature article for a magazine with some new insight into the subject of your book and with something useful for the magazine's readers. Try to time this to coincide with the publication of your book. You can't buy publicity like that.

- Accept speaking engagements and arrange for your current book, or a selection of your books, to be available for sale at the meeting you've been asked to address. You sell more books to a captive audience than you do at any so-called book-signing in a bookstore or shopping mall, unless your name is John Grisham or Fergie.

- If you write book reviews of other people's books as part of your cash crop income, be sure you are identified as the author of your newest book, with title and publisher information.

- Spot possibilities for interviews and exposure in print even in tiny newspapers or on pages other than the book page. Go ahead and be brash and offer yourself to a local or weekly or special-interest paper. Print is good.

- Do the same for local radio and TV channels. You never know who is going to hear you.

- Remember two hoary clichés that apply to you and your writing:

One thing leads to another.
No energy is wasted.

PART SIX

Doing Business

In Which the Writer Deals with Deals

If you ever thought you weren't in business, now is the time to disabuse yourself of your illusions. You are a seller of words and you are about to negotiate a sale. All your preparation, your careful analysis of the market, your cultivation of the client, your display of your wares and potential, and your beautifully presented, well-thought-out pitch (aka query) have resulted in more than a nibble. You've got a deal.

The next question is, just what kind of a deal have you got? In the case of a magazine sale, you have a go-ahead. This used to be verbal, often even last-minute, a swift agreement between an editor and a writer to fill a hole in the book. More formally, but also usually verbal, you may have a specific assignment with enough time and expense money for research and sometimes travel to gather the information necessary to write it. No more. Both sides realized they had to have a letter of agreement to avoid nasty surprises later on. This simple document would spell out word count, deadline, price, and so on. The Periodical Writers Association of Canada drew up a straightforward, useful letter of agreement (or intent) which served for a time. It has been fine-tuned with the times and I have been allowed to print the newest one in the Appendix. But if you're going to be serious about this magazine business, you had better join PWAC and keep abreast of all the information and protection you will receive.

You may find it useful to draft your own version of such a letter, using the PWAC one as a model while tailoring it to your client's needs and yours; for example, you might be writing for a corporation rather than a publisher. It will save you some difficulties down the road if you are both clear about what is expected of you. Besides, it will make you look very businesslike.

As far as theatre or film is concerned, it's a more complicated world, with step-by-step agreement, and it is quite possible, at some stage, to lose control and ownership of your material. In the case of a commissioned play, payment usually consists of some sort of advance against box office, varying amounts coming due on receipt of successive drafts of the piece. The Playwrights' Guild (formerly PUC, Playwrights' Union of Canada) has standard contracts available (free of charge on its Web site) that define different types of productions and the fee schedules thereof. The Dramatists' Guild in the United States offers similar script services and contractual advice to its members. Also, the Writers' Guild of Canada (WGC) will see to it that you get a basic contract with a standard minimum payment, above which you can negotiate if you have the clout or a good agent.

I'm going to take you through the basic terms of a book contract because it contains all the fundamental elements and issues that a writer should be aware of. If you need help, and you will, ask your agent, if you have one, or engage a lawyer with the specific expertise. In the case of a book publishing contract, members with specific questions can contact The Writers' Union of Canada for free (but limited) advice.

Before we start, you must give a thought to what you're getting into. No matter what the job, this is, after all, a business agreement. You cannot claim any special treatment or forgiveness for your artistic oddities or failing. You are going to deliver a clean, accurate, presentable manuscript researched and written to the best of your ability, on time, and in whatever form required by your client: one or two hard copies, a disk in an agreed-upon program, illustrations, graphs, permissions, and so on, cleared and prepared by you.

Cheer up; you're about to make your mark.

AGENTS

One of the most popular workshops at any gathering of writers is the one on agents. Do you need an agent? How do you find one? Is an agent worth the commission? What exactly does an agent do for you? The relationship between agent and writer rapidly develops into something like a marriage, or it should — at least a marriage of convenience. Well, maybe it's not a marriage, maybe it's a symbiotic relationship. If it doesn't work, it can be hell.

I pointed out when I was discussing the writers' marketing directories that some of the big (American) magazines no longer consider unagented material. Too bad, because most of them don't pay enough to warrant an agent's bother. In a country like Canada, writers can usually sell their work and make a modest-to-decent living without an agent. (Define decent.) It can be done. However, they find it harder to sell outside the country because their contacts don't reach that far, nor does their expertise with all the different media that exist now to purvey their work. Younger writers coming up know already how important an agent can be to their future. In fact, it's often very difficult these days for an unknown, struggling writer to get published or produced without an agent. At the same time, agents balk at the idea of taking on a struggling, unknown, unpublished writer.

An agent is supposed to sell and promote your work, find new markets, get you bigger advances and better contracts, and suggest new projects or new uses for old product in case you run short of ideas or inspiration or income. All this takes time, which means money. In return for these services you sign over 10, 15, or 20 percent of your revenues. Note this usually means *all* your revenues unless you have some prior understanding. My arrangement with my first agent allowed me to keep all my theatre earnings and magazine fees because I did the selling. Can you find all the skills for all genres in one agent? Not likely. You'll find that most agents specialize in one field, so it's not uncommon for a successful writer in several fields to have several agents, or at least two. Anyway, first you have to convince an agent that your work will actually generate some revenue. How do you do that? You do it by getting published.

Once you have an agent, note this: your accounts statements and royalty cheques, if any, go to the agent first, that is, on any contracts he or she negotiated for you. Not only that, this is forever, or until you regain copyright to the work(s) in question, which means they have been remaindered and/or are out of print. Even if you change agents, the contracts your previous agent worked on stay in that office. You would be well advised, therefore, to stay on polite terms with all your agents, both past and present. You should expect very clear statements and accounting from your agent. Copies of all the statements from the publisher/theatre should be passed on to you. If you have any questions or corrections, ask immediately. If you have any problems with the publisher/producer, let your agent know. This is when it's very comforting to have someone fight your battles for you.

Only after your statements have been examined by the agent do you receive a photocopy of them and a cheque, if one is appropriate, less the agent's fee and GST, of course, and less, also, all the agent's (long-distance) phone calls on your behalf, faxes, photocopying, mailings, courier fees, and so on. Another hidden cost. I have begun to resent the fact that while writers charge and receive a (too small!) flat fee for services rendered, plus GST, with an expense account for research allowed only in special cases and by negotiation, most writers' helpers (agents, lawyers, accountants) charge and receive their fee plus all the concomitant costs of conducting the helper's business. In other words, you're paying their office expenses and no one pays yours.

Is an agent worth this cut you take in revenue? Writers' most common complaint about an agent is that they do all the work while the agent takes the commission. In many cases, this seems to be true, and it's something I have complained of, too. Most writers are, in fact, their own best salespersons, before and after the fact. I mean, no one can sell your work to a publisher better than you, the writer, just as no one can hustle it better after it's published, the latter activity being clearly your job. It stands to reason: no one knows your work as well as you do, no one believes in it as much as you do, no one can think of more angles to work, ears to catch, buttonholes to twist. However, few writers can fight for themselves, fight for more money, that is, or hack their way through the thicket of a contract. This is where agents come in very handy. They can bargain better than the writer and strike more advantageous deals. They have more legal expertise than writers and much thicker skins, at least to begin with. As you progress you will develop not only a certain familiarity with a contract, learning what you like and don't like, and finding out what is and isn't negotiable, you will also add layers of epidermis to your sensitive feelings. Until then, you may well be dependent on an agent.

Agents act as a kind of buffer, as do the publishers' acquisitions editors, which enables you to work with your editor on an intellectual level. I have found the same to be true of theatre work: you (or your agent or your lawyer) will work through the contract with the business manager or the company's lawyer and you will fight through the script with the director. In the past, magazine contracts have been fairly simple and straightforward, but now electronic rights are buzzing through our heads, causing headaches I will discuss later. In any circumstances, try not to bring hard feelings to the editorial table. Both you and your editor/director may thus be more amenable to each other's suggestions. Peace in our time, or at least on time.

And if not peace, maybe some help if things go wrong. Ideally, agents should be there with advice and soothing oil if the deal goes bad. Again, it depends on the agent. These are things you have to find out the hard way. This is where schmoozing comes in handy, keeping an ear to the ground, listening to the gossip and finding out who's naughty or nice.

You'll want to find an agent who's on your side, not only encouraging and optimistic about your worth but also on your wavelength. It's always nice to be understood. It's also nice to discuss the future — yours — in positive terms. Successful agents, of course, are much in demand. Be sure that yours isn't so popular, with such a large stable, as to be too busy to give you the attention you deserve. You would like to receive regular reports on how the peddling of a new work is going and what the next moves should be on its behalf. Some agents worry they will hurt their writers' feelings if they report rejections. I think most writers would rather know the worst. Even a nibble that turns out to be no bite can be nice to hear about. Hope springs.

If you haven't a new product for your agent to sell, it's still a good idea to touch base regularly. Perhaps you can meet to sound out an idea you've got simmering, to see if there's a market for it. If you're dry or broke, perhaps your agent can come up with an idea, a job that you might be able to do quickly for some fast cash. Here again, this person should know you and not offer you something you would hate to do. The relationship between agent and creator can be a tender one; it should be satisfying for both of you.

LAWYERS

Some writers prefer to use a lawyer rather than an agent. That way, they figure, they pay once for the contract work and not forever through the nose as they would with an agent who is extracting that blessed commission from every royalty cheque. Certainly, if that's all an agent does for you, the contract hassle, then you'll feel better if you stick with a lawyer — with an expertise in publishing, please, but also the entertainment business: theatre, television, radio, film. Can you find all these skills in one lawyer? You'd be surprised. These days lawyers seem to be more versatile than agents.

Before you consider hiring your own lawyer, do not underestimate the legal and contractual assistance you can receive from the various writers' organizations. Once you qualify for membership, you can join WGC and for dues, which vary annually, based on your income from Guild contracts, plus a percentage deducted from each contract payment, you get any number of services, which include bargaining and contract assistance, an RRSP account, life insurance and dental insurance, and so on. The contract department is invaluable in protecting your rights, standing firm on a basic, minimal contract with signators, below which you cannot be screwed.

WRITERS' ORGANIZATIONS

For magazine writers, the Periodical Writers Association of Canada (PWAC) offers bargaining clout and current information. You'll be advised of the basic fees, new markets, and the continuing contractual battles over electronic rights. With your membership material you'll receive a copyright kit including a model publishing agreement (letter of intent) for magazines and for Web sites. You can photocopy these or type them into your computer and keep as templates to use with potential employers. This material is backed by the expert advice of the staff and fellow members as well as a grievance committee that will offer not only advice but also protection or protest in case of an argument or problem between you and a client.

The Writers' Union of Canada also provides a grievance service and offers basic contract assistance free to its members. Be sure to get a copy of the Model Trade Book Contract to use as your basic guideline when hammering out a contract. The Canadian Authors' Association, while worthwhile and interesting, doesn't offer the same professional assistance. This is serious business.

THE CONTRACT

A contract is the main reason you need an agent or a lawyer to save you from penury and despair. Someone has to guide you through the minefield.

I will take you briefly through the basic elements of an agreement between a writer and a purchaser of the writer's work, in this case, a book publisher, so you will know what to expect, but do not by any means consider yourself qualified thereafter to read, understand, negotiate, or sign one of your own without further expert assistance. Most of the general substance applies to all contracts, be they for books, plays, or TV and film screenplays.

A contract starts out very simply and it looks nice, not only businesslike but kind of reassuring as it identifies the partners in the deal and the deal under consideration.

WHEREAS the Author (that's you) has written, compiled, or edited, or is engaged in writing, a work (the "Work") tentatively entitled:

TIPTOE THROUGH THE MINEFIELD

and the Publisher has undertaken to publish the Work on the terms and conditions herein contained:

NOW THEREFORE it is mutually agreed between the parties as follows:

And after that your complications begin. The headings are usually quite standard and generic, but you must read them carefully to determine what your responsibilities are and what are those of your publisher (or theatre, or producer).

- The initial GRANT OF RIGHTS is okay.
  That's what you both have in mind, to publish a book (produce a play/movie) of yours. But then you are expected to grant other stuff, additional and subsidiary rights as "hereinafter set forth." Like what?

  Well, in the first place, that you wrote the thing, that is, the words are yours, and you are the sole owner of the rights you're selling them. Not hard.

- AUTHOR'S INDEMNITY
  After all that, it's up to A to hold P harmless in case of damages or costs arising from a lawsuit.

  This means, if you can't say anythin' nice don't say nuthin' at all, and for God's sake be careful. The various settlements and provisions are described in succeeding paragraphs. The costs, you will not be surprised to learn, are all to come out of A's royalties.

- OBLIGATION TO PUBLISH

Notwithstanding, even although, and nevertheless, P can decide not to take the risk of publishing/producing if A's material is too iffy. If A refuses to delete offensive material or to make revisions, then P can terminate the agreement, and, depending on the contract, you may have to pay back part or all of whatever advance money you have thus far received.

- DELIVERY OF MANUSCRIPT

Yes, well, no problem there. I've already suggested you should never miss a deadline. The secret of meeting deadlines, of course, is to have good work habits and a good sense of timing — that is, an accurate estimate of how long it's going to take you to write the piece — as well as a fear of bankruptcy. You blithely promise a word count, having no idea how many words you will write, and an index due within x-number of days of receipt of the second proof pages. Failures of delivery of anything will be punished with loss of royalties, a deduction or return of the advance, depending on the lapse involved.

One of the reasons I adhere to the agreed-upon date so slavishly is that I have long since spent my advance and couldn't possibly afford to return it. For heaven's sake, be realistic in what you agree to. If the deadline looks impossible, say so right away. Give yourself and your publisher a break. Better an agreed-upon delay now than an anxious, unforeseen one later.

You also usually agree to supply photographs, illustrations, graphs, whatever, as well as permissions for quotations or material from other sources you have used. When I'm doing a cookbook, I request the publisher to furnish the illustrations — and the translation to metric measures. When I'm doing a lot of permissions (as in the book of quotations I did), I ask for more time, because other people are slow to respond. If you supply your own photographs, you'll have to nag to get them back.

- PUBLISHER'S UNDERTAKING

Now we come to the point where P has to do something for A. P agrees to publish the work within twelve (12) months of its acceptance of a final, satisfactory manuscript — and with any luck, by that time you'll be long gone and working on something else.

In the case of books, P, of course, decides about format (hardcover or paperback), cover design (sometimes you can arrange to be consulted), marketing, distribution, price, and so on. Of all the books I have written, I've actually managed to change a cover design once. Occasionally I hit with a title but more often not, and in one particular instance, a bad choice on P's part cost me and P lots of income. I don't want to talk about it.

- EDITING AND PROOFS

Past a certain point in a book's gestation period, nobody's supposed to change a thing, other than the usual nitpicking corrections. All the way along there are deadlines for return of the edited copy, then of page proofs, and so on. Usually the delays are elsewhere and by the time you receive the manuscript, you are expected to make up for others' lost time and return it in an hour. If you have too many corrections (in excess of 10 percent of the original) or decide to rewrite the book, you have to pay for it. That's why you should be very careful with your work. Anything slipshod gleams like a bad deed. Have your second, third, and fourth thoughts *before* you hit the galley stage.

My advice, at least with non-fiction, is that if you have that many afterthoughts, you should write another book. I read that Alice Munro once decided at page-proof stage that one of her stories wasn't quite right and pulled the book. She paid for the cost to the publisher; when the book finally met her standards and was published, it won a Governor General's award. Sometimes, it's worth taking a stand and fighting for what you believe in, but you have to be very sure and you have to be prepared to pay for it, because you must realize that this kind of delay costs P, who is on the hook with the advance, fixed costs for design, typesetting (or whatever it's called now), overheads, and so on. P's bankers are no more understanding than A's when it comes to shortfalls of revenue; in fact they are less so, because bigger sums are involved. Remember, we're all in business. No quarter.

- COPYRIGHT

This clause establishes in whose name the work will be held, that is, copyrighted. Unless you're using a nom de plume or are incorporated, it will be in your name. If you have a co-author, it will be in both your names. If you have an introduction written by someone else who is entitled thereby to an agreed-upon percentage of the royalties, then the introduction will be in this person's name; the same is true for an illustrator, if any. When you publish in a magazine, you usually sell first North American rights — or used to — and are protected by the magazine's blanket copyright for the entire issue. If you want these rights back to sell again, a simple letter of request returns the copyright of your material to you.

Complications arise with electronic rights and I'll get to that. As for play rights, anything that happens to a (new) play of yours during rehearsals, with your consent, belongs to you, to use or not as you see fit, and your contract should make this clear. Some directors now want credit for their input, but are getting no sympathy from the Playwright's Guild of Canada or the Dramatists' Guild in the United States. Some theatres, too, are asking for a percentage of future box-office royalties because of their kindness in mounting the first production. Do not sign a contract that requires this kind of lien on your future.

As for your use of others' words, you are responsible, as mentioned above, for getting the permissions from the publishers, agents, or authors. If you fail to do so and are guilty of plagiarism, action can be taken in the writer's name. I hope the writers I have paid to quote in my time have received their percentage from their zealous publishers. This is another chapter.

- ADVANCES

For books, an advance is a nonrefundable payment made against royalties (unless the contract is terminated), or for agreeing to do a job in the case of a business-writing contract. If the book doesn't earn out the advance, you don't have to pay the publisher back. Only when royalties surpass your advance do you earn any further money on it. My editor tells me that the standard formula for an advance is 50 percent of predicted royalty earnings in the first year. Say P hopes to sell 3,000 copies in the first year. A book priced at $22.95 (paperback!), of which A's cut is 10 percent, will earn $6,885 in royalties. A's advance will therefore be between $3,000 and $3,500. Bear in mind that 5,000 copies constitutes a best-seller in Canada and wonder why any of us remain in this business.

I must admit I wonder. The perception of wealth and fame that attaches to a published author is a myth. And yet a book proves something, that you are a "real" writer, that you stayed the course, that you are an expert in something, that is, if it's hardcover. Is it worth it, worth the time and effort? I think I'm still earning twenty-seven cents an hour. I will never, of course, quit writing. Die first.

In the case of theatre, advance payments are against projected box-office royalties, which are usually 10 percent of the gross, less for a smaller house, or the house may even pay a flat fee per performance. These are for professional productions; amateur productions pay less, a small flat fee per performance.

With screenplays or TV movies (MOW aka Movie of the Week), advance payments, payable in installments on receipt of subsequent drafts, are also against a payout, usually 4 percent of the total budget of the film, payable on the first day of principal photography, less what has already been paid. This isn't quite as pie-in-the-sky as it sounds. The budget may be very low, in which case you get nothing more. At almost any given time, once your next agreed-upon level of writing is done, the script may be taken away from you for someone else to work on and you don't own it so no one owes you another cent. Feel lucky if you get a writing credit.

- ROYALTIES

Now you start getting into numbers and this is where you establish your potential income. An agent or lawyer or contract adviser can help you here, particularly if you want to negotiate beyond the industry standards. You agree to a certain percentage of P's list price on the first x-number of copies (usually 5,000) and to more thereafter, the percentage going up incrementally according to the number of copies sold. The higher percentage will not apply to smaller print runs but there will be provisos to prevent P from doing nothing but smaller print runs. For books sold at deep discount — special sales to businesses or for bulk sale or to book clubs — a different rule and percentage will apply, usually pegged to the actual amount of money P receives. The exception here is in the case of a sale pursuant to a large initial prepublication sale.

Take, for example, the sale of my book *Beginnings* to the Canadian Life and Health Insurance Association, or the sale by award-winning fiction writer David Carpenter of his fishing guide to Canadian Tire stores. If you're into non-fiction, you would be well advised to take note of possible special sales and do what you can to help sell your book outside of the usual shelves. Also, be aware of the power of backlists — books that outlast the wear-dated labels that most booksellers seem to put on them. Make sure your publisher, that is, your publisher's sales reps, keeps pushing your perennial book and keeps it blooming on the shelves season after season.

Other book sales include those resulting from coupon advertising, radio and television ads, direct mail, and so on. As you might expect, there are no royalties payable on copies sold below cost or given away for promotional purposes. This includes copies that you request to give to enterprises or individuals you think might do the book some good. This does not mean your aunt Fanny who can buy her own copy, although she's probably waiting for you to give her one for Christmas.

I usually give away a lot of my books at Christmas, copies I have been allowed to purchase, according to my contract, at a 40 percent discount, plus GST, and on which I receive no royalty. Civilians always think you get unlimited free copies because you wrote the book, but the publisher paid to have it published so you have to pay the publisher for any further copies you want to give away. I know of writers who buy boxes and boxes of their books at their authors' discount and then turn around and sell them at full price at readings and speeches and appearances, pocketing the profits. This may sound like a good idea but there are two things wrong with it: one, you have to do the book-keeping on this and figure out what your income was on the sales so you can give the government its cut — income tax and GST. Don't you hate paperwork? Two, strictly speaking, also according to most contracts, you're not supposed to do this. It's called cheating, and you're not being fair to booksellers who are trying to make a living by selling your books.

The right of P to withhold a reasonable percentage of the royalties payable to A in anticipation of the return of unsold copies of the Work by retail or wholesale customers has always struck me as outrageous, but it's one of the nasty facts of life in the world of book retailing. It starts back with the booksellers, who buy on consignment and who are allowed to return the merchandise they don't sell. All publishers are in this bind and have recently been grievously damaged by the mega-book-stores' practice of taking huge quantities of books and then returning (or losing) them, also in huge quantities, which has left some publishers bankrupt and authors without royalties.

In any other business, retailers (or wholesalers) take their chances. They buy too many Nehru jackets or left-handed egg-beaters or purple striped sheets and they have to put them on sale, mark them down, unload. They are not allowed to send back the merchandise. Only in the publishing business. You can't blame the publishers for not wanting to pay you money they have not confirmed as earned. However, in the case of a direct and final sale, as of a special bulk purchase by a business with the money in hand and no returns possible, this should be taken into account. I have had it written into one recent contract that when my percentage on the amount received for a special sale comes to $500 or more, my royalty shall be paid immediately without making me wait until sixty days after the next account-ing. (Getting the publisher to honour this agreement is some-thing else; they say it's too much bookkeeping.) If you think you have a potential bulk sale on your hands, keep this in mind.

- ROYALTY STATEMENTS
With or without a cheque, if you have royalties coming to you, you will receive a statement of the sale activity of your Work(s) by P during the accounting period in question.[10] With all the returns and specials and percentages withheld,

---

10 The Writer's Union has devised a simplified report template for writers to request their pub-lishers to use. (See Appendix)

and so on, these statements are often hard to read — another reason to have an agent to help you until you understand it. Then when you do, read carefully because you will sometimes find discrepancies, as I have, that your agent overlooked. Never throw away a statement. When in doubt, consult your agent, if you have one, or call the royalty department of the publisher for a full explanation. The more calls P receives, the greater the incentive to produce royalty statements that even the fuzziest-brained A can understand. Write down the explanation on paper and store it in a safe place because you'll probably have to refer to it again.

- GOODS & SERVICES TAX

  It took a while for them to learn, but most Canadian publishers finally have a clause in their contracts about the GST, which you must collect to pass on to the government. If they don't, remind them, and make sure it says plus, not including. If you happen to acquire an American agent, it would be easier and less hassle for both parties if you receive all the GST and take care of it from this side of the border. That way the foreign agent doesn't have to worry about the Canadian government's taxes.

- WORK TO AUTHOR

  Contracts vary as to how many free copies are given to A: five (5), six (6), ten (10), or twenty (20). No matter how many, if you're like me you'll buy and give away lots more. My husband used to say about theatre tickets that if you give a person freebies once, you've made a friend; twice, you've made a bum. I've made a bum out of a lot of my friends and all my relatives but I honestly doubt that most of them would own any of my books if I didn't give them copies. As to whether or not they've read them, I don't ask. You'll also want to give a copy to people whose help you have acknowledged. Your publisher will usually pay for these, and mail them, if you give them the names and addresses and sign the books. It's good public relations.

- SUBSIDIARY RIGHTS

  This is where you need really expert advice. Most publishers have their own definitions of subsidiary rights; they also have their own idea of what is due to them and it seldom matches yours. In essence, P acts as your exclusive agent in the disposition of any subsidiary rights you have granted them, including first serial right and second serial rights for prepublication, condensation, syndication, selection, anthology, and abridgement, also translation, English-language publication outside of Canada, and premium or commercial usage (by licensing of a special edition). Then there is calendarization to consider, as well as poster and other merchandising rights. Book clubs are included, and audiovisual and large print rights, and the all-confusing, all-encompassing electronic dispersal, information storage, processing, transmission, and retrieval systems. The latter deserves a separate discussion and chapter — and several books!

  If you have an agent or a lawyer, P will get fewer rights or smaller percentages on the rights granted. If you have the time and contacts outside the country, you may opt to try to sell some of these rights yourself, or your agent will. I had an agent who consistently withheld foreign rights, although unable to sell much outside Canada. Later contracts in which I allowed foreign sales to be negotiated by the publisher resulted in sales to Australia, Italy, and Germany. I certainly didn't have the contacts to make this happen. You can see that there is something to be said for P's efforts on A's behalf.

  Movies are hot right now and Canadian agents are pushing Canadian books, if not into production, at least into options, which make a little money even if the material is never translated to the silver screen. Again, this kind of negotiation is something an agent can do for you that you can't do for your-self. But take note, and retain as high a percentage of the film rights in your publishing contract as you can. You never know.

The percentages assigned to P and A vary in each category. Obviously, there has to be something in it for P to hustle on behalf of your work. On the other hand, your goal is to keep as much as you can to yourself. You'll be grateful when you're old and grey and nodding by the fire if you have enough money to buy a stick of wood for it. You don't want to burn your books.

- OUT OF PRINT

Oh, we're going to get awkward again. The line in front of me reads:

> If at any time after one (1) year from the date of initial publication of the Work by P the Work shall be Out of Stock, Out of Print, and no longer for sale in Canada, in any edition, through P or through a licensee, A shall give P written notice.

Written notice of what? That the book is out of stock and you want it back in stock or that you want the copyright back. Not the easiest thing in the world. Most Ps seem to like to keep A's book a secret (frequently in more ways than one!). You'll be lucky to find out the size of the print run. As for keeping track, your best bet is to phone the warehouse and ask the Keeper of the Computer how many copies of your book are in stock. The answer may not reflect the true situation. Perhaps it seems to be out of stock, but this may be only temporary, until copies return like homing pigeons from the booksellers when they shed their unsold consignments, or perhaps P is dismayed at the book's activity and decides to dump it. If you have some inkling of this, you can beat P to the draw by asking for the return of the copyright before you are asked how many cheap (remaindered) copies you want to buy. Sometimes your asking such a thing causes P to review the sales figures and hang on to the book. What happens more frequently is that sales and your hopes dwindle before the numbers of books do. In this case P decides to do what is called ...

- REMAINDERING

Allowing for those blessed returns, plus a more or less informed scanning of the account statements, you'll already have some idea of the future of the book. Still, it's always a shock when P — well, not P but S (for secretary) — calls and asks you how many copies you'd like to buy before it's remaindered. Although your contract says that you are supposed to be given notice in writing and allowed one month to decide what to do, that is, how many copies you want to order at the low low price of $1 (usually), you will probably find that once set on your demise, P can't wait. Not once but several times I have been phoned and told to let P know within twenty-four hours. Not nice.

When this happens be sure to retrieve your copyright. Get a release in writing and file it with the original contract. (One publisher recently started to charge $1 for this service.)

VIGNETTE

The story is true, told me by the man himself, of the efforts Wayne Dyer (*Your Erroneous Zones*, *Pulling Your Own Strings*) made to drag his ailing first book onto the best-seller lists. He took out a bank loan to buy up the remaindered copies and stored them in his basement, setting his wife to work on a mail-order campaign to all the students he used to teach at an eastern college — Michigan, I think — offering them a chance to buy the book. He loaded the back of a van and conducted his own little promotion tour. He'd wheel into a town, book himself onto the local television station for an interview or onto an open-line radio show to offer free advice. Then he would find a bookstore and offer the manager a percentage of the sale of his book if Wayne could direct his listeners and viewers to come in for a signed copy. It worked.

When Dyer's publishers saw the increasing sales on the selling charts, they went for a second print run[11] and the rest is a mystery because the books are early New Age, mom-and-pop psychology, and not even very well written.

Failing a basement or a wife or both, you might have difficulty emulating Dyer's sales approach, but his aggressive marketing strategy is worth noting. Much simpler for you to make every effort on your own behalf, introducing yourself to booksellers wherever you may be and offering to sign copies of your book in stock, and encouraging them to be embarrassed if they've sold out and not bothered to replace it/them. You should also remind your publisher's promotion and sales people where and when you will be speaking, reading, or appearing in another city and available for a little gig on TV or radio. Then arrange to have books on sale at the event or make sure the local bookstore is well stocked. Help your publisher and yourself by making special sales happen. You cannot afford to hide your light under a bushel, but sometimes it takes a peck of work to keep it burning. Your aim is to keep that book in print and make sure it's on the shelves of the bookstores, not the warehouse.

Current contracts allow only twelve (12) months from the date of initial publication before P can remainder your dreams.

---

11 Dyer didn't say, but if the book had been remaindered, the publishers would have had to buy back the rights. I know because this happened to a book of mine when a publisher decided to go for a new edition and had to renegotiate.

Earlier contracts used to allow more time, when they specified at all, but there are more books being published now and each one's shelf life must be limited. Cottage cheese!

- AUTHOR'S PROPERTY

  In this clause P promises to take care of your stuff, any photographs, documents, charts, illustrations, artwork, whatever, that P borrows, but not to the point of worrying about it. Fire damage or other accidental destruction doesn't obligate P to do a thing. You'll be lucky to get your pictures back. Help P and yourself by supplying a list of the material you expect to have returned. By the same token, keep solicitous track of anything you may have borrowed and be sure to return it. Do make sure you recover the original manuscript. You might want it some day for archival reasons, so it's up to you to keep track of your data and to remind the editor what you need back as soon as the book is on its feet. I knew one writer who used old galley pages to write letters on, but fewer and fewer people write letters now so this may not appeal to you.

- SUBSEQUENT EDITIONS

  Nowadays you have to agree to edit and revise your book for second or subsequent editions without any further advance. As sales continue, you will get royalties down the line, but often you will encounter a lean period as you put in borrowed time, energy, and research in the hope of future sale. In cases like this, you need more than hope. You need a line of credit to buy time, coffee, and copy paper. If you're lucky, or un-, that is, if the revisions account for more than 20 percent of the original text, you will receive an advance against further royalties. A revised book is like a part-time job — a lot more work than meets the eye. You know the old rule: work expands to fill the time allowed for it. Make sure you budget enough time for it.

- COMPETING WORK

During the term of this Agreement, A shall not publish or permit to be published, distributed, or sold, any full-length written Work using the subject matter of the Work as its basis in a manner which is going to affect the sales.

The idea is not to compete with yourself or to adversely affect the sales. Of course, you can't sell the same book to another publisher. But a small spin-off can help you, if you work it right. I deliberately try to sell something related to the Work to appear in a magazine just around pub date in order to increase the sales. You can sell yourself, you just don't sell a reworked chapter. Write something fresh, tailored, of course, to the magazine's audience, but on the same topic as your Work. So, too, with speeches, readings, whatever else that is related — you're not exactly a toy tie-in for sale with every Whammy Sandwich, but you are a saleable commodity, for a while. It's all promo.

- NEXT WORK

I try always to cross out the clause that binds me to submit any future proposals, giving P right of first refusal before soliciting offers from other publishers. At least now the refusal is usually given a time limit of three weeks. I wrote too much to tie myself, even for three weeks, to any one publisher. Watch it. Mind you, I've known writers who get around this by submitting impossible ideas with what they think is an absolute guarantee of failure and rejection. Reminds me of the movie *The Producers* (1968), in which in spite of all their efforts to fail, the producers of a Broadway show had a hit on their hands.[12]

---

12 In real life, as well.

- TERM OF AGREEMENT
  This clause simply describes the length and validity of the Agreement and the contingencies by which it may be terminated (bankruptcy, other defaults) and the conditions under which A can buy back at cost all the material relating to the publication of the Work, if it's still available. Lots of options and grants still hold, however, so be aware. It's a marriage after all, and divorces are painful.

- REPROGRAPHY
  This clause deals with what is already happening in Canada: both A and P may (and have been doing so) license Access Copyright (formerly CanCopy), the Canadian copyright licensing agency, to administer photocopying and other reprographic rights in the Work on behalf of both A and P. You are also allowed to authorize Access to authorize [sic] reproduction for Braille or visually impaired users. I don't, but you may be nicer than I am.

  The Canadian National Institute for the Blind (CNIB) used to squeeze a concession in individual contracts for such use of the Work. My argument, in agreement with TWUC, is that if CNIB pays its janitors, who have to earn a living even if their employers are blind, then it can pay writers too for the same reason.

- ASSIGNMENT
  This is where you are reminded that everything you do is serious and permanent and even if you aren't around to honour your commitment, your successors, heirs, and estate will have to. After a recent fiasco in Canadian publishing, everyone got very sensitive about the assignment of rights. Do not give P the right to abandon you and sell his rights in your work out from under you. And don't think that you are going to get out of your obligation by dying. The best revenge is writing well.

The last few pages of a contract are housekeeping, mopping up loose ends and making sure everyone is paying and will pay proper attention. They may include headings like these:

- ARBITRATION
- FURTHER ASSURANCES
- REMEDIES CUMULATIVE
- NOTICES

The interesting thing about NOTICES is that they recognize the legally binding aspect of a fax transmission. Snail mail is okay, too, albeit rather slow.

- ENTIRE AGREEMENT

That's all, folks, but not quite. You are reminded that the agreement is governed by

- PROPER LAW

and that all those cute

- CAPTIONS

which I have copied are not a part of the Agreement, as such, and not to be considered as serious explanations. When in doubt, consult your friendly neighborhood lawyer.

- IN WITNESS WHEREOF

et cetera et cetera, and I would like herewith to thank Pamela Jordan and Joyce Lusk, my mail persons in MacTier, who have witnessed many documents for this solitary A.

PART SEVEN

Owning Up

*In Which the Writer Acts Possessive,
but not Paranoid*

COPYRIGHT, A HISTORY

In late October 2002, Access Copyright officially opened for business with a party celebrating its new Web site and its new name. This new on-line Rights Management System (RMS) is the culmination of years of work that began back in 1988 when the first substantial revisions to Canadian copyright law were enacted since it came into force in 1924 (legislated in 1921). It authorized the establishment of collective societies, enabling the collection of copyright fees on photocopied materials. The original collective agency was called the Canadian Copyright Licensing Agency (CanCopy) and it set the machinery in motion for collecting those fees. Shortly thereafter The (short-lived) Electronic Rights Licensing Agency (TERLA — later subsumed into CanCopy) was also formed to collect licensing fees for the electronic use of the creations of Canadian writers and artists. Did I say culmination? It's just the beginning.

Writers have always worried about the theft of their intellectual property and they have a lot to worry about now. It's a whole new world out there, the most major upheaval in the history of the dissemination of thought since the Gutenberg printing press. This revolution is only possible because of the computer, and/but the solution is implicit in the problem — a database that boggles the mind.

The first time I heard that phrase, *intellectual property,* I was excited by all it implies. The idea that something I created, made up out of thin air — well, out of words on paper — constituted an *entity* that I *own* was staggering. A brass widget is concrete; anyone can see it's a brass widget and that someone made it. If a customer wants one, he buys it; if he wants another one, he buys that, too. Everyone understands that. A combination of words, on the other hand, seems to most people to be an abstract thing, and besides, it's so easily reproduced, copied, quoted, keyed in, downloaded, printed, and reprinted that it hardly seems to belong to anyone any more. So what's all the fuss about?

It's about your work, about having the product of your efforts recognized and the use of it paid for. For that matter, writers have to understand this basic concept as well. When they do, they will finally and fully realize that they are, in fact, in business, in the manufacture and sale of unique combinations of words. Anyone who tries to use their property without paying for it is guilty of theft and is breaking the law.

The thing is it's so easy to steal on-line. Material is just there for the downloading, just floating up there in cyberspace until you pull it down and print it on your own paper in the privacy of your home. Privacy, yes, but also piracy. Again, you ask, as an innocent user, what's all the fuss about? Ah, but what if the words being pulled out of the ether are yours and what if you are receiving little or no compensation for them?

Who steals my purse steals trash. Who steals my words steals cash. Remember that. Your copyright is your right to be copied and to be paid for being copied. You had better understand what's involved. It wouldn't hurt for you to look up the Canadian Copyright Act on the Net and read it over. Failing that, or also, join PWAC, if you're eligible, and get a Copyright Kit from them. You can buy other useful professional information from TWUC for nominal prices (see Appendix for list). So I'll just hit the highlights and hope they illuminate enough to send you in the right direction.

The basic point is that you own everything that you write, from the moment you write it down. You don't have to register it, publish it, or send it out, but if and when you do, you are allowed to license your work to another party (magazine or book publisher, etc.) for publication or production; that is, you authorize copying, usually in return for some pay. This is true in Canada as well as in the United States.

There are some significant differences between Canadian and American law that you would be wise to learn. If you sell your work in the United States, you are protected there under the American copyright law, and you may find the U.S. Copyright Office useful.

Both countries protect the same kinds of creations and grant similar rights to their creators, but there is a more forgiving and freer use of copyright material under American laws than under Canadian. Even if your work is published in Canada but distributed in the Unites States, you are subject to American laws, just as American creations are subject to Canadian copyright laws when published or distributed in Canada.

Amendments to the Copyright Act were proclaimed in 1997, and though it still grants a creator's writing fifty years' protection following death, this now includes *unpublished* work as well. Not great. Previously, unpublished material was protected until it was published and then protected for fifty years after that. So what happens to memoirs, diaries, letters, long-lost manuscripts, and so on that only come to light years after a writer's death, or that have had a moratorium laid on to protect the privacy of relatives? Although unpublished, these documents have no longer protection than published work.

Apart from this, as I said, your copyright protection in Canada does not depend on formal copyright registration; it simply exists. You will be pleased to know that your book publisher automatically includes a copyright notice in your books, in the name stipulated in your contract. You book will also be assigned an ISBN (International Standard Book Number), which facilitates inventory control and order fulfillment.

Periodicals have a copyright notice in each issue that offers you a blanket protection in Canada. Beware of the little magazines and local weeklies that accept and publish your work for little or no money; they often do not post a copyright notice. You're okay in Canada but not outside the country. (I've had work of mine published in such a little magazine taken for nada, translated, and produced on radio in Iceland! At least my name was used, which is how I learned about it; I have a cousin in Reykjavik who heard the story.) If you feel a modest little rag is the way for you to break into print, copyright the material yourself.

Speaking of periodicals, however, PWAC is a little wary of Access Copyright. The problem, of course, is distribution. It is theoretically easy to track the use of a writer's work in book form if it has an ISBN, but what of the vast repertoire of short stuff in magazines, journals, and newspapers? I suppose this is part of the reason that many newspapers so fiercely guard their archives, as opposed to their current databases, and that the outcome of the lawsuits is so vital to them. It's even more vital to writers. Oh, it's worms-within-worms-within-cans thereof!

At the time of writing there are two outstanding class action suits in English Canada by writers against newspaper publishers over the electronic rights to their work. I won't go into detail here; it's going to be a long time before settlement is reached. Briefly the point of the argument is this: the newspapers want electronic as well as print rights to the writers' work for a one-time payment (or a minuscule pittance for on-line rights) for work the writers have done for them. Unaccountably, writers expect to be paid. Can you imagine? A landmark case in the United States (Tasini vs. *The New York Times*) that found for the writer may establish a precedent that will help Canadian writers to restore their rights and bring them (slightly) more money.

None of this will cost the consumer more, by the way. The big media already charge for downloads and database access. I tested this by applying to *The New York Times* for an article I wanted to read. I went to the archives, found it, paid $2.50 American for the right to download and copy the material. It's very easy — too easy. All writers want is that the big guys share the proceeds. There is, however, a certain amount of effort required of writers: they have to furnish the inventory. As I say, it's not as easy as referring to an ISBN. I think we accept as only fair and logical that readers pay us for the right to read our work and we, in turn (like everyone else), pay other writers for the use of their property. We have to be vigilant, however, to protect our copyrights from any inroads or exemptions being foisted upon them.

I recommend to your devoted attention Canadian lawyer Lesley Ellen Harris, an international expert in copyright, licensing, and e-commerce. Her articles and papers are published worldwide and she is the author of a book called *Canadian Copyright Law* (third edition, 2001). Check out her Web site in the Appendix and do consider taking her on-line course on copyright law and check out your rights for yourself. You can't go blindly into those good rights.

While you're at it, give a thought to —

MORAL RIGHTS

Moral rights are an important part of your copyright, having to do with your very essence. You retain moral rights to your work even after you have sold the copyright to it.

The best example I can give you of moral rights being flouted was a publicist's application of red ribbons to the necks of the geese flying in the big atrium at Eaton Centre in Toronto. The group sculpture was created by Canadian artist Michael Snow; when he saw the arbitrary use of his art in a Christmas promotion, he sued and won the right to the purity of his work. The ribbons came off. You might call that a moral victory.

Creators can agree (be persuaded) to part with their moral rights, to bend them or not to exercise them. Briefly, moral rights have three general categories:

- right of paternity,
- right of integrity, and
- right of association.

Paternity has to do with your child, your work. You have the right to claim your work as your own, or not; that is, you have the right to use a pseudonym or remain anonymous (but still own it). *Integrity* has to do with your honour and reputation. A work may not be violated or distorted or changed to the detriment of honour and reputation (e.g. with red ribbons) without your explicit consent. Putting altered words in your mouth can be very unhygienic and you have the right to prevent such alterations. The *right of association* enables you to prevent anyone from using your work to sell a product, service, cause, or institution to the detriment of your honour and reputation. (Do you want your novel's heroine to be emblazoned on a T-shirt?) (For how much?)

PLAGIARISM AND PERMISSIONS

TALE

The classic example of envious plagiarism involves Oscar Wilde and James Whistler. Whistler said something witty. Wilde said, "I wish I'd said that," and Whistler said, "Don't worry, Oscar, you will." I have also heard this attributed to Oscar Levant, which just goes to show you.[13]

American novelist Thomas Mallon wrote an entire book about plagiarism, *Stolen Words*, which includes a capsule history of plagiarism as well as specific larcenous examples. He comments that the history of copyright actually has more to do with piracy than plagiarism. That's what we have to understand. It all began, as Mallon points out in his book, with the printing press. When words could be reproduced, their ownership could be acknowledged but the words could be stolen, and the ownership contested.

In the olden days of troubadours and minstrels, oral tales were not only treasured but repeated. When/if the lays were written down, the tales, though not the telling, were written in stone, embedded in memory as they were; creativity lay in the graceful telling and word choice but very little in ideas or character development when a consciousness of self did not even exist. (The very concept of self can be traced to the printing press and the development of literacy.)

Once words became accessible to a larger audience than present company during the telling of the tale, their value increased. "Let me tell it" gave way to "I said that" and the teller wanted more than a good dinner and a place to stay the night. Once the printing press arrived and words were copied in numbers greater than a hand with a pen could achieve, they became a saleable commodity, and readily available to others with pencil, pen, or press. And so the literary copyright — the right

---

13 The late Canadian writer W.O. Mitchell once said to me when I said something witty that he would give me credit three times; after that it was his.

to copy — was conceived. The first copyright laws began to be enacted in England in the sixteenth century, according to Mallon, though initially it was the Crown's method of controlling seditious or heretical material.[14] Not until the eighteenth century were the rights of authors finally recognized in the Statute of Anne (1710), paving the way for the concepts of "literary work" and "the author," ideas we take for granted.

By now we all assume the right of the original compiler of the words to be recompensed for the use of a specific arrangement that we have learned to call in this context *intellectual property*. It's a question whether redneck governments and rapacious reprographers do. Unless you're criminal by nature, you wouldn't dream of stealing your neighbour's property; his pig is his own thing. Well, thou shalt not covet thy neighbour's words nor can you freely use them. Copyright laws recognize the ownerships of words and remind you that you are larcenous if you steal them. I hope my repetition has made this abundantly clear.

Copying rights are a blessing or a nuisance, depending on which side of the page you're on. Yes, of course, plagiarism is an outright felony, but how do you protect yourself from what American novelist Nicholson Baker has called "verbal poaching"? And how do you avoid doing it yourself, even inadvertently? "The price of eternal vigilance," said the Canadian media guru Marshall McLuhan, "is indifference," but I think he was mistaken. The price of eternal vigilance is eternal vigilance. In other words, you can never let down your guard. Even as you are so vigilantly protecting your own words, be just as careful not to steal other people's gems of wisdom and jewels of phrase without due acknowledgement and, in some cases, recompense. It can cost.

When I was working so long and hard on my book about women's diaries,[15] I joked one day to my publisher that I could write a whole collection of women's words about men just from my own library of female writing. "Do it," she said, and I did,[16] easily, in my spare time,

---

14 This and the following information from an essay, "Purloined Letters," by James R. Kincaid, *The New Yorker*, January 27, 1997.

15 *Reading Between the Lines: the Diaries of Women* (Toronto: Key Porter Books, 1995)

16 *Men! Quotations about Men by Women* (Toronto: Key Porter Books, 1993)

until it came to gathering up the permissions for the use of other people's words. Then I had to write a veritable blizzard of letters enclosing the copy I was using and requesting permission to do so. Learn from my efforts and errors.

Some intrepid people assume that the use of two hundred to three hundred of other people's words is acceptable without formal permission. It is not. You must be more careful and be sure to ask. Under the rubric of fair use,[17] only the following acts of copying are not considered to be an infringement of copyright: for the purposes of private study; research; criticism or review (where the criticism is accompanied by sufficient acknowledgment of the work); or for news reporting in a newspaper, magazine, or periodical if the source is indicated along with the name of the author.

As you can see, quoting from someone in a book such as this one, which is mostly by me, and which would exist without that someone's words, is a little different from quoting someone in a book entirely dedicated to the sayings of other people. One might be a substantial use — "significant and qualitative" — while the other is apparently less so, but no matter whether you're taking a sentence or two from a large book or quoting a line or two of a poem, which is usually only thirty-some lines long, you must seek permission. And if you're quoting from a song, which is also short, you will discover that it's fiercely protected by the most powerful copyright protective agency in the world, the Association of Songwriters, Composers and Publishers (ASCAP) in the United States; the Society of Composers, Authors and Music Publishers of Canada (SOCAN) (formerly CAPAC) in Canada; and various other acronyms in other countries, all affiliated — symbiotic, you might even say — with *microfiche* power to the nth degree. Depending on what you quote, how it's used, and who it's from, you will be charged a fee. In some cases you can bargain; in others you can't, but according to your contract with your publisher, you'll be

---

17 "Fair use" is the American term; "fair dealing" in Canada is similar but not identical. Let your conscience be your guide and take careful note.

responsible for clearing permission and you have to decide how necessary the quotation is to you.

Public domain, of course — a work that has passed the period of copyright protection — is generally fair game, but not always. If the words have been brought to light by the assiduous study of a writer or editor, then they might conceivably be copyrighted and you will have to acknowledge that. Sayings attributed to public personalities and celebrities, usually from newspaper interviews, may also be used for free, and duly attributed, but beware. I have seen clever lines by celebrities that were actually cribbed from writers. And look at the confusion between Lily Tomlin and her writer for many years, Jane Wagner: one of them said the words, the other one wrote them. Did you know that the reporter owns the transcript of an interview — actually owns the words?!

There are other exceptions to what you think is public domain. Sometimes, as in the case of a translation, even of an old work, the translator holds the copyright to a new translation and you may need to ask for permission to quote from it. When in doubt, check the translation. Sometimes an editor has cleaned up material — changed it to modern spelling, put in some punctuation, made sense of the chronology, and so on — so thoroughly as to have a copyright claim. Sometimes, as I recently discovered, a protective association has taken over the care and surveillance of an author's work after legal protection has run out. There is, for example, a foundation watching over the use of the poet Kahlil Gibran's words (perhaps trademark rights? For profit?). It all depends on the circumstances. Take a careful look at the copyright or other intellectual claims in the front of the book you want to use, and, as I keep saying, be careful.

When you write for permission to quote, you must give the title of your projected book, the name of your publisher, the number of pages, print run, price, distribution (Canada? North America? World?), and the planned publication date. This last will help speed the reply, but point it out and ask for prompt handling. Enclose with the letter a copy of the page or pages from your manuscript on which you have used material by the writer in question.

Remember scavenger hunts? Some of this apparently simple operation turns into a maddening search for a writer or a publisher. Letters come back with the publisher's address unknown, or the reply that the author has left for another publisher, with or without rights, with or without a forwarding address. You may be told to try the author's agent. In some desperate cases, after a six-letter search, you may be lucky enough to be given the writer's home address. The nicest, most generous replies, I have to tell you, have been from other writers who never charge and who always reply to my friendly, chatty request with some friendly chat of their own.

Some writers do not wish to be quoted, not even for ready money. Agents for Marilyn French, Erma Bombeck, and Adrienne Rich, for example, refuse to grant permissions. Others, through their publishers, want more than they're worth to you. Camille Paglia wanted to charge more than Gloria Steinem or Margaret Atwood and I balked.

While my quotation book was still malleable, I could refuse to pay what I considered an exorbitant fee and delete the author's line(s). Once the book had gone to press and a slow reply put me over a barrel with a request for payment, I resorted to bargaining, begging for leniency, often citing the discrepancy between the American and Canadian dollar as a reason for giving me a break. Usually this worked and I paid a little less. In the end, my permissions cost me about $1,000, a limit I had set myself when I started out. I didn't count my postage, paper, or time.

It's a little easier, as I say, when your own material comprises the bulk of the book and you need to ask for only a few permissions of minuscule size. Still, it's wise to err on the side of caution. When in doubt, ask. If, after all your efforts, there are still people or publishers you have been unable to find and whose permission you have not managed to obtain before your book is published, be sure to publish a disclaimer in your acknowledgements, saying that you have made every effort to locate the sources, and you would be only too happy to hear from people and recognize them in the next print run.

ELECTRONIC RIGHTS

Well, you say, I've already written something about electronic rights; why beat this electric horse? Believe me, no matter what I say, it's never enough. As the patron saint of Canadian writers and the official lawyer for The Writers' Union of Canada, Marian Hebb, writes in the *Writers' Guide to Electronic Publishing Rights*:

> The Writers' Union of Canada recommends that writers do not grant the right to publish in electronic form nor the right to sublicense electronic publishing rights when signing a book contract with a publisher.
>
> Writers should retain all electronic rights to their work and only grant electronic rights on a project-by-project basis.
>
> In other words, negotiate and sign a separate agreement directly with an electronic publisher for a specific use which is described in that agreement.

This directive is a little longer than Strunk and White's famous dictum in *Elements of Style*,[18] but you should try to commit it to memory, or hang it up by your desk for a daily reminder. The little booklet contains a Draft Checklist for Electronic Publishing Agreements which you should enter into your hard drive, with several back-ups.

POEM
'Mid pencils and palimpsests
Where ever I may roam,
No matter where I download
There's no page like home.
— ME

---

18 "Omit needless words. Omit needless words. Omit needless words."

Writing in *The Sunday New York Times* magazine about electronic rights and the cavalier treatment thereof, James Gleick[19] expressed writers' resentment of the civilians who have been trying to rob us, commenting that our opponents "tend to be people who never actually tried to make a living from their writing." This complaint, of course, applies to anyone who tries to steal our intellectual property; information highway robbery is really photocopy felony raised exponentially.

I'm trying to keep this discussion generic to avoid instant obsolescence. I've enclosed lots of signposts to the highway in a bibliography of URLs at the back of the book. Follow the links, try to keep an open mind, and remember to smile, or at least grimace. As Stephen King said, you don't want to lose your soul in a "pot of message." Although today's technology may be obsolete yesterday, writers, I hope, will not be. McLuhan, thou shouldst be living at this hour!

Let's get back to basic copyright. Once one's work was safely stowed on paper in library shelves, giving others access to them, for a price, how could money and immortality fail to follow? Such was the thinking of the naïve writer on first breaking into print. As more and more people learned to read and demanded more and more material to fill their heads, or pass the time, the future looked very bright for any writer. Unfortunately, people learned to write as well as read, and a lot of them wanted to sell their words, too. Levels of expertise and areas of interest proliferated, with words and audiences enough for all, or so it was thought. Today we're beginning to wonder if there are too many words and not enough audiences. We are in danger of being crushed by books.

Ah, but wait! A whole new audience is rising. The screens of the world's computers comprise a vast new maw voracious for product. Words can bypass paper now, flowing into our awareness on a digital highway that acknowledges no bounds of country, customs, tax, or fee. Readers can browse to their eyes' content (or detriment) and download or print at will, committing to their own paper the words and ideas (and

---

19 Author of *Faster: The Acceleration of Just About Everything* (New York: Pantheon Books, 1999)

images and music and films) of strangers. How will those strangers be paid? Does anyone care?

Writers do.

A TALE

My son John is not a working writer. He is a physicist, a teacher, a computer guru, and he climbs mountains for fun. He wrote an article that was published in *Quantum* magazine about the physics of climbing: thrust, pressure, stuff like that, with awesome equations and a lovely picture of him in a mountain chimney.

Someone — in Colorado, he thinks — took the time to enter his article on a home page and it went around the world. John has had e-mail from Russia, Australia, and all over commenting on his piece and he has enjoyed hearing from the people who read his story. I was appalled. He hadn't been paid another penny for the distribution of his work. He didn't care. He had a day job.

That was my first encounter with the mind-boggling free electronic dissemination of words. After that first shocked awareness came the grim realization of the media's attempts to abrogate writers' rights on the Net. The fight has just begun.

And so, Access Copyright. We live, we hope, not only in a just society, but in a collective one.

PART EIGHT
Leap of Faith

*In Which the Writer Comes
Face to Face With Self*

The Final Truth

Process is everything.

That's all? After all this preamble this is all I have to say? Trust me. It's profound. As you get older and realize that the brass ring is receding faster than your hairline, you must have found your ultimate, lasting justification in the sheer joy of writing.

One of the great, hidden, unsung blessings of writing is that you find out who you are. Discovery is daily, not necessarily pleasant, but always remarkable. And so you remark. Some of your remarks are remunerated, some are not. They are no less useful to you, though you can't buy bread with them. You see, in the end it doesn't matter whether you are a success in the eyes of the world. You are writing. You write, therefore you are. Writing, that is, creation, continues to be the most challenging, terrifying, wondrous act you can imagine. Don't stop imagining.

Process is everything.

The Support System

The professional organizations and associations working in your field are valuable assets. You will have noticed how often I mention one or the other of them in the course of other discussions, and I have appended a list of some of them with their addresses. I recommend joining one or several of them as soon as you qualify for membership. The one deterrent may be the cost of memberships, especially if you cross genres with your writing and are eligible in several different disciplines. Then it is a matter of choosing which organization will be the most useful to you, not forgetting what you have to offer in return. Although most of them have a paid director and (small) staff, none of them would function without the volunteer work and support of their members — you, me, us.

In addition to occasional discounts and excellent information, most professional associations offer other financial services you would be well advised to notice, including, with some, health benefits or insurance (disability) plans, and they're working towards group Registered Retirement Savings Plans. Contract assistance for a price is no longer available from TWUC to non-members, but it still provides some one-on-one advice to members. Still, there are excellent resources available, including the Union's Self-Help Contract Package (see Appendix). Most writers' associations also have grievance committees, giving assistance and advice to members having trouble with their publishers. This kind of informed help with some clout behind it is especially valuable now in the light being cast from computer screens around the world as they download purloined words.

When you qualify for membership in a professional peer group, do investigate the services and perks being offered, being aware also of the bargaining power you buy into with your name and dues.

Until you have a book committed for publication you will likely not have a professional editor. However, you may be able to find other part-time or amateur editors along the way: gifted friends who may also be writers, gifted readers who may also be friends, gifted actors (if you are a playwright) who may be good critics, or a gifted group (people in a good writing workshop) who may possibly cause more pain than you care to suffer. A lot of writers belong to a writers' group, guild, or workshop. There are probably almost as many writing groups as there are curling clubs or bowling groups in small cities across North America, and they serve a wonderful purpose. But do be careful; your creation can be workshopped or analyzed to death if you don't watch out.

Writing workshops are like dream-analysis groups. Sometimes they tell you about your dream and they're right on; you feel it in your gut. Other times what they tell you is utter nonsense and you wish they'd go away. Go with your gut. If a comment gives you a wonderful shock of recognition, a sudden insight that illuminates what you're doing and solves a problem, then it's probably right; at least you can use it. If no one turns on a light, then have a glass of wine and leave. Find another group.

Ultimately, you will have to become your own best editor. Consider editing simply another one of the modes you will fall into, using the left, as opposed to the right, side of the brain. Gabriele Rico tells us in his book, *Writing the Natural Way*, "The right hemisphere ... can create designs with images, recognize patterns of sound, reach out for metaphor, and play with recurrences, juxtapositions, and ambiguities, enabling us to make the rich and evocative patterns that give life to natural writing." You know that already. I'm talking abut the left side now; if you never let the left hemisphere know what the right hemisphere is doing, you're going to get into trouble, also debt. It's low time for you to make that left side work for you as well. (High time is for the fun side.) One of these days, you keep saying, you have to get serious. That day has come. But it doesn't mean that you have to face it alone. No one can work in a vacuum.

MENTORS

Struggling young writers are not struggling with their writing. They're not short of ideas or skill. What they really want is an encouraging word and maybe a bit of intellectual hand-holding. Enter the mentor. Everybody ought to have at least one. Of course, you assimilate all you have met and you have no qualms about picking people's brains if they warrant the picking, but you also have to be very careful of what people tell you, as I have just indicated re workshopping/dream analysis. Keep some thoughts to yourself, also reservations. Some words of wisdom work better than others and are also easier to understand. The people who first told me that I needed a retreat to write in and offered me theirs knew what I needed before I recognized it myself. People who tell me to stop writing so many different things don't understand how hard it is to earn enough money as a freelancer.

You don't want to be misled or unduly influenced. I've have people advise me what they would do rather than what I should do. Some would-be critics are like that too, analyzing the play they would have written rather than the one I wrote. I have made some damaging errors following the advice of people I respected, but of course I should have known better — or sought a second opinion. I'm not alone. You hear of classic cases like Svengali, who completely controls his tone-deaf singer, Trilby, who has no career without him.

My first mentor was Chester Duncan, my advisor for my master's degree at the University of Manitoba. He was an expert on W.H. Auden (my thesis subject), not only a professor of English but also a composer of music, with impeccable taste in both fields. I still do not forget what he said to me when I graduated: "I expect you to be public." A mentor should be challenging. Ches is gone now, but he remains a touchstone for me, and for many others.

Your best bet is someone in your field, or in a closely related field, that is, creative. Because theatre is my first love, I enjoy talking to actors and directors and am grateful when we can share insights. A couple of each have been very helpful along the way.

I had a very pedantic friend, an entertainment lawyer, who was a stickler for correct pronunciation, accurate diction, and cogent grammar. We could not be together for longer than an hour without arguing about some point of language. Fortunately we were each right about half the time so we remained friends. When I was in doubt about a word, I could get an answer faster from a phone call to him than from a search among my dictionaries. He died a few years ago and I still miss his nitpicking. He was by way of being a mentor.

One of my best mentors is a man, younger than I, whom I met about twenty years ago at, appropriately enough, a writers' retreat. At that time Richard Teleky was managing editor of Oxford University Press, Canada, but I have known him first and always as a writer and he is now an award-winning published author. His first response to me was as an editor. He commissioned me to write a cookbook (*The Betty Jane Wylie Cheese Cookbook*). He also signed food critic Joanne Kates, whom he met at the same retreat, which just goes to show you that you never know when or where you're going to meet someone who offers you a job.

Over the years Richard and I have read and criticized each other's fiction,[20] and I have tried to help him in whatever way I can in return for his advice and insights about my career. He has been responsible for a lot of my decisions and has caused me enormous amounts of work, most notably my book *Reading Between the Lines*, which had its beginning over a coffee conversation when he suggested since I was so interested in diaries, why didn't I write a book about them, thereby changing the course of my life. Like that. He's busy now and I miss him.

Mentors are not easy to come by, nor can you program their arrival. Serendipity has a lot to do with finding someone on your wavelength but it helps to be in the right place at the right time and to be receptive. The search for a mentor is one of the strongest reasons that would-be and hopeful writers attend writers' conferences, seminars, and workshops. Like little kids lining up with an apple for the teacher, they bombard the exhausted creature after hours in what is a tightly packed schedule, offering drinks, meals, and rides in return for one-on-one advice and continuing attention. My overburdened heart goes out to them because I've been on both sides of these pressure groups.

If you as a mentee feel a need to continue the contact with a writer-teacher — or a writer-in-residence — after the sessions are over, stop and consider what you are asking. That person is trying to make a living too and cannot easily give you free advice. Unthinking words don't take much time but informed advice does, and that time has to be productive for all concerned.

Brace yourself: as a writer-teacher, you'll get fan letters from your groupies after a conference is over. I was brought up to be courteous, as I've said, so I always answer my mail, but I can do it in a polite but perfunctory way, subtly discouraging further communication. Some people, as you'd expect, don't take a soft answer for a no and keep bugging. If you are the

---

20 I must be among the very few people who have read his unpublished novels.

one bugging, go back to that secret of always starting a letter with *you*. Stop and consider what, if anything, *you* can offer your mail-order mentor.

Information, for one thing. Marla Hayes, one of my mentees in North Bay, where I taught twice, five years apart, at a summer arts course at Canadore College, offered me some addresses of possible markets I didn't have, references to articles I had missed in a useful journal she subscribed to, with subscription information, plus friendly but inexorable chat to which I finally succumbed. When she asked me to read a script for her and to comment, I did, without charge. She has become a friend and I give her freebies, but she doesn't presume, nor do I with my mentors.

Another legacy from another incumbency, Kat Fretwell, a poet who lives nearby, relatively speaking, is about the closest thing to a fan I've ever had and calls herself one. I've given her critiques, happy to do it because she was being ripped off by a so-called poetry consultant who was charging her an exorbitant $50 an hour without ever picking up on her wavelength. I mention this because there are self-styled mentors out there who are no help and who will cost you too much. Professional mentors have their place but be sure they're worth the price.

I have been blessed in my mentors. My friend and mentor, the GG-award-winning poet Don Coles, has read my poetry and given me the benefit of his sharp intelligence and generous evaluation, in addition to springing for the cappuccino. Once on extremely short notice when a publisher wanted to carve up a very long poem of mine, he replied by return e-mail with some helpful solutions. Richard Teleky has also edited my poetry, but now, as I break into film, cut to screenwriter DONALD MARTIN, a new friend and mentor with an eye for a scene and an ear for a line.

Professional Mentors

For those of you on the advising end, who may want to continue a working relationship with a mentee, consult the going rates and charge your client fairly and accordingly. Actually, I never have, but the threat of a fee is enough to make unwanted clients go away. They can't seem to understand that I was being paid for the time and attention I gave them while I was a resident writer, and that when I'm on my own again I'm still trying to earn my living.

Others feel the same way. Enter the professional mentor.

Another idea whose time has come — and gone? — in these parlous times, the paid mentor replaces the kindly professor, the mesmerizing Svengali, or the demanding editor. I actually participated in such a project a few years ago and found it factitious. You can't legislate rapport; it's chemistry. Or not. I took part in the first year of a three-year pilot program administered by the Writers' Union for the federal Human Resources Department; a similar program existed in the League of Canadian Poets. The Cultural Human Resources Council (federal) still runs a kind of mentor program but it's strictly a youth service.

The way it worked then, for writers, was, as I say, an arranged symbiotic relationship between an experienced writer and a promising one. In return for a (welcome) stipend, "successful" (define successful) writer A will tell all to hopeful writer B just starting out on that street of dreams. It's show-and-tell time on a one-to-one basis, a bit like what I am doing here. Perhaps this book will stand in lieu of a paid mentor, offering all the if-onlies from wherever you're standing:

> MENTOR: If only I had known what I know now …
> MENTEE: If only I knew as much …
> MENTOR: If only I were as talented, or young …
> MENTEE: If only I were as skilled and as wise …

You can see it's a bargain fraught with possibilities.

I applied to be a mentor and was accepted, assigned to a young (early 20s) writer named Michael Coldwell, who was already a published author of two young-adult novels, one of them an award winner, and with a contract for a third. It was not an entirely successful relationship. Michael was very busy, not only with his third book but also with an alternative and beguiling career in promotion. He said in his application that he wanted to learn more about career and business management, marketing and promotion — all skills he has been employing ever since, but not for his writing.

It took a number of phone calls to track him down to where he lives now in Las Vegas where he has a full-time job with one of the major hotels. He did finish his third YA novel but didn't want to continue in that vein. He has written an adult novel, he says, and one screenplay, but has done little to market them, being too busy marketing others. He apologized to me for our aborted relationship, said he didn't feel he gave enough. I felt the same way, actually. I think the point is that you can't legislate these things.

The fact is that although every writer needs a mentor they come only through serendipity, or perhaps through a writer-in-residence program. I've picked up a few mentees that way myself. Before I begin such an incumbency now I say I'm like Velcro and I wonder who will stick. As the saying goes, a stranger is a friend I haven't met yet. Well, now you have me and this book. Use it/me well.

TAKE TWO ASPIRATIONS AND CALL ME IN THE MORNING

Most writers need more than one lifetime to express all their ideas. The trick is to make a living during the lifetime they have. I've talked to young writers who are already despairing, without hope or expectations of living fully by their wits. One of them, not even all that young any more, said that after ten years of writing with a modicum of respectable success, he still can't afford to quit his day job.

It's the system. I was arguing for a larger advance with one of my publishers at about that time and he told me I was the only writer they had in their stable who expected to make a living by writing. Mid-list, middle-aged, middle-class, respectable writers are being overlooked now for the blockbusters, the sure-fire megahits that will soar on the charts and crush the also-rans. On the other hand, the really young ones, hearts afire and burning with energy, are being kindled by agents who see a long career ahead of them. No one ever said it was easy.

These are chronic problems of writers, not likely to go away; in fact they will probably get worse as the attrition of grant money continues and publishers cope with their current debacle, cutting back their lists, decreasing their advances, and in some cases going bankrupt and shutting up shop. Magazines go belly-up and theatres close their doors. These days, everyone, not only writers, seems to be working harder for a smaller share of the pie. How small can it be cut?

"The number of sacrifices I make keeps on escalating," another writer said to me, "to the point where I have to sacrifice my writing."

The horror of this kind of sacrifice is that no one will ever know. If you don't write something, or if you write something other than what you wanted to write, just to make ends meet, then no one will ever see what you might have done. (Some day, when you have time, I'll tell you about all my fish-that-got-away.) It just doesn't exist. But you do. You have this rich, secret inner life that you keep nurturing any way you can. You must never let go of the process.

A PARABLE WITH A COUPLE OF MORALS

In Alison Lurie's novel *Real People*, a modest, middle-class married woman with one small, respectable book of short stories to her credit goes to an art colony to work on a new collection with the approval of her husband, children, and mother. After a toe-curling affair with a sculptor, she realizes how safe she's played it, not censored by her family but by herself for fear of rocking her little boat. An older writer who is trying to finish a novel before she dies of cancer tells the younger woman a truth she learned too late: You don't get a second choice. You must choose what is most important to you and then live with it, for good or ill.

My case proves that this is not entirely true. I was thrust by circumstances into a second choice. My husband's death forced me to make writing my first choice for survival, if not for art. I didn't have to feel guilty any more, worrying that I was neglecting my duties for writing. Now my duty *was* writing, and the necessity of making it pay our way. But then other choices had to be made and they are part of the problem of making a living as a writer in this day and age and country and climate of thought. Too often my choices were expedient. Although I have never written anything repugnant to my standards, I also have had little opportunity of letting the world go hang for the sake of my aspirations. The alternatives were clear: write or get a day job; publish or perish. It takes faith, hope, and chutzpah, these three, but the greatest of all is chutzpah.

Remember what Samuel Johnson said: *Sir, no man but a blockhead ever wrote except for money.*

Is there anything you'd rather do?

APPENDICES

MODEL LETTER OF INTENT
For First Serial Print Rights Only

(Type this form into your computer as a master standard letter and modify as needed for each assignment. Send the resulting letter to your client before you begin work. That way there will be no nasty surprises when your client receives your invoice.)

DATE:

Dear _____:

It is a pleasure to be working with you. My understanding of our agreement is as follows:

I will write an article of (insert number of) words, on (insert description of assignment). I will deliver the article to you on (insert date) via (hardcopy/computer disc/e-mail) in (insert computer program) format.

I understand that you will pay me (insert amount) per word/a flat fee (insert amount)/a rate of (insert amount) per hour to a maximum of (insert amount), and that such payment will be made within 15 days of my delivery of the article. I also understand that you will notify me in writing within 15 days of my delivery of the article whether the article is acceptable or requires revision; otherwise the article shall be considered accepted by you.

I will be pleased to provide up to (insert number) rewrites, as required. Please forward a copy of any changes you make to the article prior to publication.

License of North American First Serial Print rights in English shall commence on my receipt of payment. The license shall be limited to (insert one: the day of publication/30 days/6 months/12 months).

I understand that in the event that the article is unacceptable and it is deemed rewriting would not render it acceptable, we have agreed on a kill fee of (insert amount, ideally 50 percent of the total fee). If, however, the article is not published for any other reason, the entire fee will be due and payable. If you do not publish the article within 12 months of delivery, I will have the option to revert the rights without penalty.

You may store the article on your database for legal and historical archive purposes only, and not for resale. I retain all other rights to the article, including reprographic (photocopying), database, CD-ROM and all other electronic rights. If you wish to use the article in any way other than is allowed via North American First Serial Print rights in English (for example, on your Web site, or on an electronic database), I will be pleased to negotiate terms with you at that time.

OR, substitute the following, where appropriate:

The license to publish the article on your Web site (the name of which is [insert], and the URL of which is [insert]) shall commence on my receipt of (the agreed) payment. The license shall be limited to (insert one: the day of publication/30 days/6 months/12 months).

Sincerely, et cetera.

Prepared by the Periodical Writers Association of Canada

Be sure to check with the PWAC Cope Kit for other model letters and useful information.

STANDARD FREELANCE PUBLICATION AGREEMENT

Periodical Writers Association of Canada

STANDARD FREELANCE PUBLICATION AGREEMENT

This agreement is between _____("the Writer")

and _____("The Publisher/Client")

Description of Assignment: _____

Working title: _____

Byline to read: _____

Source of idea ("Writer" or "Editor"): _____

Approximate length of article: _____

Deadline: _____

Tentative publication date: _____

Print rights licensed (check):
    One-time Canadian First Serial Rights _____
    One-time North American First Serial Rights _____
    English Language: _____
    French Language: _____

Fee for print rights licensed: $_____

Web site rights licensed:

The right to publish the work in the original language on the following Web site:

   Name _____ URL _____

Such right is (check one)
   exclusive _____ non-exclusive _____

And is granted for a period of (check one)
   24-hr day of publication _____
   7 days _____
   15 days _____
   30 days _____
   3 months _____
   6 months _____
   1 year _____

After which such right (check one)
   becomes non-exclusive _____
   reverts to the Writer _____

Additional fee
For Web site rights licensed: $_____

General expenses: The Publication agrees to reimburse the Writer for direct expenses incurred in fulfilling this agreement. Such expenses shall include photocopying, fax, long-distance telephone calls, Internet charges, couriers, and _____

Such expenses will not exceed a maximum amount of: $_____

Travel expenses: The Publication agrees to reimburse the Writer for travel expenses to a maximum amount of $_____. Travel expenses will include: _____

The Writer agrees to write, and the Publication agrees to publish, a manuscript in according with the following Terms of Agreement. This agreement includes any attached materials initialed by both parties. The fee specified in this agreement does not include Goods and Services (GST) or other applicable national or provincial sales taxes.

_____ Date:_____
(Publication representative)

_____ Date: _____
(Writer)

TERMS OF AGREEMENT

Part I: THE WRITER'S OBLIGATIONS

1. Truthfulness and Accuracy

   1.1   The Writer will not deliberately write a dishonest, plagiarized or inaccurate statement into the manuscript. The Writer shall reveal any conflict of interest or possible conflict of interest to a representative of the Publication, hereinafter called Editor, upon receiving the assignment.

2. Sources

   2.1   The Writer will be prepared to support all statements in the manuscript and to assist the checker in verifying statements of fact.

   2.2   In stories involving trials, public hearings or other controversial disputes, the Writer will try to check all sources against a transcript of the proceedings, if one is available.

3. Libel

   3.1   The Writer shall alert the Editor to special circumstances regarding a story that could present legal risks to the publication. In the case of a libel action, the Writer shall support the Publication morally and by appearing for the defense, if requested.

4. Deadlines

   4.1   The Writer shall deliver a clean, typed or word-processed manuscript on or before the agreed deadline. If the writer cannot meet the deadline, the Writer shall give the Editor reasonable notice in advance of the agreed deadline. The Writer may not set a new deadline without the Editor's permission.

4.2   If the Writer fails to complete the assignment on deadline without the editor's agreement to an extension, the Editor has the right to terminate this agreement and owe the Writer no further payment.

4.2.1   If the article proposal originated with the Editor, the Publication has the right to pay a kill fee in accordance with Section 15 and receive a copy of any draft manuscript and copies of any research material the writer obtained. However, payment of the kill fee does not give the Publication the right to publish the manuscript.

5. Revisions

5.1.   The Writer and Editor will discuss the content, style, research, focus and point of view to be used in the manuscript. The Writer will then use his or her best efforts to write the manuscript within the agreed parameters and will obtain the permission of the Editor before departing from any of them

5.2   If the manuscript, as submitted, fails to fall within the agreed parameters, the Editor may require the Writer to revise the manuscript. The Writer and Editor will agree on the suitable time for making these revisions.

6. Updating

6.1   If delays in publication or changes in the circumstances surrounding a subject make extensive update of a manuscript necessary, the Writer will update the manuscript, for a fee to be negotiated, if his or her other commitments permit.

6.2   If unable to update the manuscript, the Writer retains his or her rights under Section 12.

7. Editorial Changes

7.1 The Writer will be available for discussion and consultation during the editing process.

7.2 The Writer will notify the Editor in writing if, after reading the final edited version of the manuscript, he or she wishes to withdraw his or her name from the manuscript before its publication.

8. Expenses

8.1 The Writer will not incur any extraordinary expenses without prior agreement of the Editor.

8.2 Within 60 days of acceptance of the final manuscript, the Writer shall claim reimbursement for expenses and/or account for any expenses paid in advance, and the Publication shall make such reimbursement within 10 days of the receipt of such claim.

Part II: THE PUBLICATION'S OBLIGATIONS

9. Sources

9.1 The Publication will respect any promises of confidentiality the Writer has made in the course of obtaining information.

10. Libel

10.1 Where advisable, the Publication will hire a lawyer to review the manuscript for libel implications.

10.1.1 In the case of a libel action, the Publication will morally support the Writer. If the Writer requests it, the Publication will pay the costs of the Writer's defense. Where possible, the Publication will provide the Writer with a separate lawyer.

11. Revisions

11.1 In requesting revisions to a manuscript, the Editor will give reasonable, detailed instructions as to the nature and extent of the required changes.

11.2 If the Editor requests revisions that involve significant departures from the previously agreed-upon approach or treatment, the Writer may refuse to revise the manuscript and still be entitled to full payment. If the Writer agreed to do the revisions, he or she will be paid for the time spent rewriting at a rate to be negotiated.

11.2.1 "Significant departures" include a) new research; b) change of focus; c) change of style; d) change of opinion or point of view.

12. Updating

12.1 If the manuscript requires extensive updating for the reasons mentioned in Section 6, the Editor will offer the Writer first opportunity to do the updating.

12.2 The Publication will pay the Writer for updating at a rate to be negotiated.

12.3 If a person other than the Writer does the updating, the Editor will give the Writer an opportunity to review the changes and to remove his or her name from the published manuscript in accordance with Section 13.

13. Editorial Changes

13.1 The Editor shall inform the Writer of changes in the edited version of the manuscripts while there is still time to discuss and reach an agreement on such changes.

13.2 The Editor will give the Writer an opportunity to read the final edited version of the manuscript reasonably in advance of its publication.

13.3 The Publication must withdraw the Writer's name for use in connection with the published version of the manuscript, if the Writer so notifies the Editor in writing.

14. Acceptance and Payment

14.1 The Editor will notify the Writer of its acceptance or rejection of the manuscript within 15 days of a) receipt of the manuscript, or b) the deadline, whichever is later; otherwise the manuscript shall be considered accepted by the Publication.

14.2 The Publication will pay the agreed fee to the Writer within 10 days of acceptance of the manuscript and will pay expenses in full within 10 days of receiving the Writer's account of expenses.

14.3 If for any reasons unrelated to the requirements of the assignment, the Publication decides not to use the manuscript, the Publication will pay the Writer the agreed fee and expenses in full.

14.4 If the manuscript is accepted by an Editor or another person with apparent authority to do so and is later deemed unacceptable, the Publication will pay the Writer the agreed fee and expenses in full.

14.5 If under this agreement the Publisher licenses the Web site rights to a work previously or simultaneously published in either print or electronic format, either by the Publisher, Writer, or a third party, such licence shall commence upon the Writer's receipt of the agreed-on Web site fee.

15. Kill Fee

15.1 If the Writer delivers a manuscript that fails to meet the requirements of the assignment and if the Publication considers that the manuscript cannot be made acceptable through rewriting, the Editor may terminate the assignment by providing the Writer with written notice and paying the Writer not less than one-half of the agreed fee, plus the Writer's expenses to date, in which case all rights to the manuscript shall revert to the Writer.

15.2   If the Editor requests a rewrite that requires the Writer to express opinions that are not the Writer's own, to include information that, in the opinion of the Writer, will falsify or distort the story, or to write a substantially different manuscript, the Writer may withdraw the manuscript and terminate the assignment. In this case, the Publication will pay the Writer no less than one-half of the agreed fee plus his or her expenses to date, in which case all rights to the manuscript shall revert to the Writer.

15.3   If, in the course of research or during the writing of a manuscript, the Writer concludes that the information available will not result in a satisfactory story, the Writer will inform the Editor and give reasons to discontinue the assignment. If the Editor agrees, the assignment is terminated. The Publication will pay a fee, to be negotiated, to compensate the Writer for work done prior to termination, on presentation of the Writer's research documentation.

15.4   If the Writer or Editor wishes to cancel this agreement after work has begun, the Publication will pay a fee, to be negotiated, to compensate the Writer for work done prior to cancellation.

16. Expenses

16.1   If no limitation is specified in writing, the Publication will reimburse the Writer for all customary and normal out-of-pocket expenses incurred in completing the assignment.

PART III: COPYRIGHT

17. Copyright in Published Manuscripts

    17.1   Unless the parties agree otherwise in writing, this agreement licenses the Publication only the rights indicated on the first page of this agreement. The Publication has the right to enter the manuscript into and retrieve the manuscript from a computerized information storage and retrieval system only for the purpose of preparing the manuscript for publication, and may store the article in its database for legal and historical purposes only. The Writer retains the copyright.

    17.2   All other rights are the Writer's exclusively. These rights include reprint rights, electronic rights, photocopying and other reprography rights, and the right to enter the manuscript into or retrieve it from a computerized information storage and retrieval system for purposes other than publication under the terms of this agreement.

18. Copyright in Unpublished Manuscripts

    18.1   The Writer owns all rights in a rejected manuscript and may submit the manuscript elsewhere for publication.

    18.2   If the Editor rejects a manuscript and pays the Writer a kill fee in accordance with Section 15, the Publication may not publish the manuscript but may retain a copy only for purposes of documenting the assignment.

19. Reversion of Rights

    19.1   If the Publication accepts a manuscript but does not publish it within 12 months of acceptance, the Writer shall have the option to revert all rights licensed herein without penalty or cost.

19.2　If under this agreement the Publisher licenses the Web site rights to a work previously or simultaneously published in either print or electronic format, either by the Publisher, Writer, or a third party, and does not publish it on its Web site with 6 months of the signing of this agreement, the Writer shall have the option to revert such rights without penalty.

PART IV: MEDIATION AND ARBITRATION

20. Mediation

20.1　When the Writer and Publication disagree over the interpretation of this agreement, they may each appoint one representative who will endeavor to settle the dispute by mediation.

21. Arbitration

21.1　When such a dispute cannot by resolved by this means, if both Writer and Publication agree, each may appoint one representative to a three-member arbitration board.

21.2　The third member, who will chair the arbitration board, will be appointed by agreement of the first two members. If the two members cannot agree, the third party will be appointed by the court in accordance with provincial laws governing arbitration.

21.3　Neither the Writer nor an employee of the Publication may act as representative or sit on the arbitration board.

22　Duties and Power of the Arbitration Board

22.1　The arbitration board shall investigate and arbitrate only those disputes that are referred to it by the Writer or Publication.

22.2   The arbitration board shall rule on the dispute by a majority vote. That ruling shall be binding on both the Writer and the Publication and is not subject to appeal.

22.3   If arbitration involves costs, the arbitration board shall rule by majority vote what percentage of costs will be paid by each party. That ruling shall be binding on both the Writer and the Publication and is not subject to appeal.

23. Action at Law Still Allowed

23.1   This part does not prevent either the Writer or the Publication from pursuing an action in law subject to the following limitation: both parties agree that once an arbitration board has been established, its ruling shall be binding in all disputes referred to it, and there shall be no appeal by either party.

AGREED AND CONFIRMED, etc. with signatures and witnesses of both parties.

ROYALTY STATEMENT CHECKLIST

You'd think that publishers, who are in the business of literate communication, would manage to issue a clear royalty statement to their authors. I am not alone among writers who have difficulty in making sense of their reports. This Royalty Statement Checklist has been approved by the Writers' Union Contracts Committee, which suggests you request that this information appear in your semi-annual (or annual) royalty statements from your publisher on books published previously or preferably when you are negotiating a new contract. You'll need it.

(The publication of this material has been permitted by TWUC. You will find it at the back of the Model Trade Book Contract brochure.)

This is the information you require for each edition (hardcover, trade paperback, revised edition) of each title.

1. Name of Author

2. Author's Agent (if applicable)

3. Royalty Period (from _____ to _____)

4. Title of Book

5. Book Number (ISBN), price, month/year of first publication and subsequent printing(s)

6. Number of Copies Printed
    This period: _____ Cumulative: _____

7. Number of Copies Shipped
    This period: _____ Cumulative: _____

8. Number of Copies Damaged
   This period: _____ Cumulative: _____

9. Number of Copies Returned
   This period: _____ Cumulative: _____

10. Number of Copies in Stock as of the End of the Period
    This period: _____ Cumulative: _____

11. Number of Copies Sold at Each Applicable Price and Royalty Rate
    This period: _____ Cumulative: _____

12. Royalties Earned (from all sales of the publisher's edition)
    This period: _____ Cumulative: _____

13. Other Specified Earnings (subsidiary rights revenue)
    This period: _____ Cumulative: _____

14. Payment Due (payment enclosed or unearned advance)

NB Reserve against returns: ideally there should be no provision in your contract for reserves against returns. If the publisher insists on including a reserve against returns in your contract it should not exceed 20 percent of the royalties reported during the royalty period and should not be applicable beyond the first three royalty periods. Reversals of the previous reserve and details of any subsequent reserve, if applicable, should be included in your royalty statement.

Check your publishers' catalogue to ensure you are being paid on the appropriate list price, as it may change from time to time.

FEE SCALE

Over the past twenty-odd years fees for writers in both Canada and the United States have not changed. The cost of food, heat, shelter, entertainment, cars, equipment, clothes, and janitorial services has risen regularly and substantially over the intervening years, but not writing. In a way, it's our own fault. Up-and-coming wannabes, so eager to be in print, will agree to anything to see their name in a byline, hang the fee.

In the meantime, even if our time and inspiration are accorded the same low payment, we have expenses that never used to exist: computers, cartridges, and disks; on-line charges and Web sites; and — still — paper and postage, to say nothing of couriers and Xpresspost. If the basic fee for periodical writing had risen by two cents per word a year since PWAC was founded in 1976 when members managed to negotiate a (slightly) higher fee range, it would be up to $1.54 per word now. Surely it is not unreasonable to set the bottom line at $1.50 per word. The bookworm has turned. It's time writers were paid a decent wage.

PWAC has published a fee scale, outdated now and under re-construction, that is, subject to imminent change. Here is my personal assessment, offered as a guideline: a fee scale for the twenty-first century, negotiable up or down depending on how humble and hungry you are. It also depends on where you live; there are regional differences in what the traffic will bear.

Periodical Writing

General Interest/Consumer Magazines
- $1.50 to $4.00 per word
- $500 to $10,000 per article
- $400 to $1,500 per column

Trade/Special Interest Magazines
- $0.50 to $2.00 a word

- $500 to $4,000 per article
- $300 to $1,000 per column

Newspaper Writing

Large Daily Newspapers
- $1.50 to $2.50 per word
- $1,000 to $2,500 per article
- $350 to $1,000 per column

Smaller Community Newspapers
- $1.00 to $1.50 per word
- $150 to $1,000 per article
- $100 to $500 per column

On-line/Web Site Writing

Varies widely; "business" sites pay more

Advertising Material

Copy/Scripts/News Releases
- negotiable

Advertorials
- $100 to $150 per hour (plus or including travel, meetings, phone calls/interviews)

Corporate/Business Writing

Reports/Marketing Plans/
Technical Writing
- varies widely
- $3 to $5 per word
- $500 to $15,000
- $100 to $150 per hour

Editing

Varies acc. to publication/project
- $100 to $150 per hour

Ghost Writing	*Articles*
	• negotiable, depending on the publishing and writing experience of the author/co-author/ghost
	• generally two to three times the usual rate
	Books
	• $25,000 to $75,000 flat fee
	• entire advance + 50% of royalties
Government Writing	*News Releases/Studies/Reports*
	• $3.00 to $6.00 per word
	• $3,000 to $150,000 per project (!)
	• negotiable
	• $150 to $200 per hour
Newsletters	*Writing only; layout extra*
	• $1.50 to $2.00 per word
	• $400 to $8,000 per issue
	• $100 to $150 per hour
Scripts	*Radio (highly variable)*
	• $75 to $150 per minute of script
	Television (highly variable)
	• $100 to $150 per minute of script
Speech Writing	• $1,000 to $10,000 per speech
	• $100 to $150 per hour
Teaching/Instruction	• $100 to $150 per hour
	• $500 to $1,000 per day

Translation/Adaptation

Literary
- $0.50 to $1.00 per word

Other
- $0.50 to $1.00 per word
- $80 to $150 per hour

USEFUL ADDRESSES AND URLS

Note that professional organizations require proof of a certain level of expertise as the criterion of membership. You join Access Copyright by signing over collective rights on your published material. The Playwrights' Guild of Canada requires that you have had a play produced in an Equity house, but makes allowances for cities or provinces/territories where there are no Equity members. The Periodical Writers' Union demands a certain number of articles/word count published in commercial periodicals; the League of Canadian Poets wants to see a published book of poetry (not a chapbook), with a minimum number of pages the bottom line. The Writers' Union of Canada needs to see a full-length book published by a recognized publishing house (not a vanity press, though the line is becoming a little blurred).

To join ACTRA you must have chalked up a certain number of points for appearances, and for the sister organization, the Writers' Guild of Canada, x-number of hours of produced scripts (television or film). The Dramatists' Guild in the United States has a two-tier system of membership: only those writers who have had a production on Broadway are eligible to be company officers. However, if you are a produced playwright, American or Canadian, you may find it's worth it for the newsletters and quarterly magazines you will receive with all their newsy items. If you join the American Theatre Guild, you will receive as part of your membership a subscription to *American Theatre* magazine and discounts on its directory and other books and perhaps a few shows in New York.

Each of these associations will supply an application form and ample information upon request.

ADDRESSES

Access Copyright
One Yonge Street, Suite 1900

Toronto, ON M5E 1E5
Phone: 1-800-893-5777
Or: (416) 868-1620
Fax: (416) 868-1621
Web site: http://www.accesscopyright.ca
e-mail: info@accesscopyright.ca (general inquiries)
licensingadmin@accesscopyright.ca (licensing inquiries)
affiliates@accesscopyright.ca (affiliation inquiries)

Canadian Authors Association
("Writers helping writers")
Web site: http://www.canauthors.org
There are branches across Canada. Try canauth@redden.on.ca and
go from there.

The Canada Council for the Arts
Michelle Legault, Lise Rochon, or Danelle Serault, Information Officers
350 Albert St.
P.O. Box 1047
Ottawa, ON K1P 5V8
Phone: 1-800-263-5588 ext. 5060
Or: (613) 566-4414, ext. 5060
Fax: (613) 566-4390
Web site: http://www.canadacouncil.ca
e-mail: info@canadacouncil.ca

Public Lending Right Commission
Web site: http://www.plr-dpp.ca
Phone: 1-800-521-5721 or (613) 566-4378

The League of Canadian Poets
54 Wolseley Street, 3rd floor
Toronto, ON M5T 1A5

Phone: (416) 504-1657
Fax: (416) 504-0059
e-mail: league@poets.ca
Web site: http://www.poets.ca

The Periodical Writers Association of Canada
54 Wolseley Street, 2nd floor
Toronto, ON M5T 1A5
Phone: (416) 504-1645
Fax: (416) 504-9079
e-mail: info@pwac.ca
Web site: http://www.pwac.ca

The Playwrights Guild of Canada
54 Wolseley Street, 2nd floor
Toronto, ON M5T 1A5
Phone: (416) 703-0201
Fax: (416) 703-0059
e-mail: info@playwrightsguild.ca
Web site: http://www.playwrightsguild.ca

The Writers Union of Canada
40 Wellington Street East, 3rd floor
Toronto, ON M5E 1C7
Phone: (416) 703-8982
Fax: (416) 504-7656
e-mail: info@writersunion.ca
Web site: http://www.writersunion.ca

The Alliance of Canadian Cinema, Television and Radio Artists (ACTRA)
(offices across the country)
2239 Yonge Street
Toronto, ON M4S 2B5

Phone: (416) 489-1311

Web site: http://www.actra.ca

(writer members belong to the Writers Guild of Canada)

ACTRA Fraternal Benefit Association

Phone toll-free: 1-800-387-8897

National Writers Union (United States)

National Office East

113 University Place, 6th floor

New York, NY

USA 10003

Voice: (212) 254-0279

Fax: (212) 254-0673

e-mail: nwu@nwu.org

Web site: http://www.nwu.org

The Dramatists' Guild of America, Inc.

1501 Broadway, Ste. 701

New York, NY

USA 10063

Phone: (212) 398-9366

Fax: (212) 944-0420

e-mail: igor@dramaguild.com

Web site: http://www.dramaguild.com

Theatre Communications Group

American Theatre magazine

355 Lexington Ave.

New York, NY

USA 10017

Phone: (212) 697-5230

Fax: (212) 983-4847

e-mail: tcg@tcg.org
Web site: http://www.tcg.org

URLs

Copyright Act
http://laws.justice.gc.ca/en/C-42/36324.html

Copyright Clearance Centre, Inc.
http://copyright.com/Rightslink/Default.asp

Lesley Ellen Harris (sole proprietor of)
http://copyrightlaws.com

Newsletter on Copyright and New Media Law
http://www.library.yale.edu/~llicense/ListArchives/9904/msg00038.html

International Federation of Reproduction Rights Organisations
http://www.ifrro.org/about/purpose.html

Repetitive Stress Injury (RSI)
http://www.engr.unl.edu/eeshop/rsi.html
— follow the links!

Keeping Steady Income (Advice)
http://e-writers.net/advice/steadyinc.html

The Canadian Association of Journalists
http://www.eagle.ca/caj/

Cultural Human Resources Council
http://www.culturalhrc.ca

World Intellectual Property Organization
http://www.wipo.org

Canadian Conference of the Arts
http://www.ccarts.ca/eng/04res/artfacts.htm

PUBLICATIONS AVAILABLE FROM TWUC AND PWAC

TWUC Publications

The following is a list of publications prepared by The Writers' Union of Canada about the business of publishing that may be useful to writers. These booklets are available upon request to: Publications, The Writers' Union of Canada, 40 Wellington Street East, 3rd Floor, Toronto, Ontario, M5E 1C7

Model Trade Book Contract	$4.00
Help Yourself to a Better Contract	$7.00
Ghost Writing (by Marian Hebb)	$6.00
Anthology Rates and Contracts	$6.00
Author and Literary Agent (guidelines)	$3.00
Writers' Guide to Canadian Publishers	$7.00
Author and Editor (by Archbold, Gibson, Lee, Pearce, Walter)	$6.00
Writers' Guide to Grants	$6.00
Awards, Competitions, and Prizes	$7.00
Income Tax Guide for Writers	$6.00
Libel: A Handbook for Canadian Publishers, Editors and Writers (by Julian Porter, QC)	$6.00

(All prices include postage, handling, and GST)

PWAC Publications
(Courtesy PWAC's Web site)

PWAC Guide to Canadian Markets for Freelance Writers
Discover new markets for your work with this guide listing more than 900 Canadian periodicals that buy freelance materials. Includes both print and online publications, contact information, submission requirements, payment rates, subject indexes and more.
PDF file: $19.26

The PWAC Guide to Contract & Business Practices for Freelance Writers
An essential resource for freelance writers. Includes information on what to charge, protecting your copyright, publishing rights and licenses, as well as model Letters of Intent and PWAC's Standard Freelance Publication Agreement.
Printed book: $21.40
PDF file: $16.05

The PWAC Guide to Editing as a Sideline for Freelance Writers
Professional writer/editor Denyse O'Leary helps you to evaluate whether editing is the right complement to your writing career. She provides valuable advice on how to obtain training, get established and set up a freelance editing business.
Printed book: $21.40
PDF file: $19.26

SUGGESTED READING

This is an arbitrary list, of course, just giving you a few of my favourites:

THEORY/THINKING

Auden, W.H. *The Dyer's Hand, and Other Essays*. New York: Random House, 1962.

Chekhov, Anton. *Notebook of Anton Chekhov.*, Tr. S.S. Koteliansky and Leonard Woolf, New York: The Ecco Press, 1987.

Dillard, Annie. *The Writing Life*. New York: Harper & Row, 1989.

Dillard, Annie. *Living by Fiction*. New York: Harper & Row, 1988.

Emerson, Ralph Waldo. *The Complete Essays and Other Writings*. New York: The Modern Library (Random House), 1940.

James, Henry. *The Complete Notebooks of Henry James*. With introduction and notes by Leon Edel and Lyall H. Powers, eds. New York: Oxford University Press, 1987.

Kundera, Milan. *The Art of the Novel*. New York: Grove Press, 1986.

Sternburg, Janet, ed. *The Writer on Her Work*. New York: W.W. Norton, 1980.

Sternburg, Janet. *The Writer on Her Work, Vol. II*. New York: W.W. Norton, 1992.

WRITING

Atwood, Margaret. *Negotiating with the Dead: A Writer on Writing*. Cambridge: Cambridge University Press, 2002.

Brande, Dorothea. *Becoming a Writer*. Los Angeles: J.P. Tarcher, Inc., 1981.

Brown, Rita Mae. *Starting from Scratch: A Different Kind of Writer's Manual*. Toronto, New York, London: Bantam Books, 1988.

Davies, Loma. *The Nuts & Bolts Writer's Manual*. Fort Lauderdale: Cassell Publications, 1991.

Evans, Glen, ed. *The Complete Guide to Writing Nonfiction*. New York: Harper & Row/Perennial Library, 1988.

Euland, Brenda. *If You Want to Write: A Book about Art, Independence and Spirit*. Saint Paul: Graywolf Press, 1987.

Gardner, John. *On Moral Fiction*. New York: Basic Books, 1978.

Gardner, John. *The Art of Fiction*. New York: Vintage Books, 1985.

Goldberg, Natalie. *Writing Down the Bones: Freeing the Writer Within*. Boston and London: Shambhala, 1986.

King, Stephen. *On Writing: A Memoir of the Craft.* New York: Scribner, 2000.

Lamott, Anne. *Bird by Bird: Some Instructions on Writing and Life.* New York: Anchor Books, 1995.

Rico, Gabriele Lusser. *Writing the Natural Way: Using Right-Brain Techniques to Release Your Expressive Powers.* Los Angeles: J.P. Tarcher Inc., 1983.

QUOTATIONS AND USEFUL ITEMS

Charlton, James, ed. *The Writer's Quotation Book: A Literary Companion.* Yonkers, NY: The Pushcart Press, 1980.

Henderson, Bill, ed. *Minutes of the Lead Pencil Club.* Wainscott, NY: Pushcart Press, 1996.

Mallon, Thomas. *Stolen Words: Forays into the Origins and Ravages of Plagiarism.* New York: Ticknor & Fields, 1989.

Norman, Donald A. *Turn Signals Are the Facial Expressions of Automobiles.* New York, Toronto: Addison-Wesley Publishing Co. Inc., 1992.

Todd, Alden. *Finding Facts Fast: How to Find Out What You Want and Need to Know.* 2nd Edition. Berkeley, CA: Ten Speed Press, 1979.

BUSINESS

Briemer, Stephen F. *The Screenwriter's Legal Guide, Clause by Clause.* New York: Dell Publishing, 1995.

Harris, Lesley Ellen. *Canadian Copyright Law,* 3rd Edition. Toronto: McGraw-Hill Ryerson, 2001.

Hill, Bonnie Hearn. *The (Expanded) Freelancer's Rulebook: A Guide to Understanding, Working With and Winning Over Editors.* Ashland, OR: Story Line Press, 2002.

Larsen, Michael. *How to Write a Book Proposal.* Cincinnati: Writers' Digest Books, 1985.

Parker, Lucy V. *How to Open and Operate a Home-Based Writing Business.* Cincinnati: Writers' Digest Books, 1995.

Perkins, Lori. *Getting an Agent: The Definitive Writers Resource.* Cincinatti: Writers' Digest Books, 1999.

Russel-King, Caroline and Rose Scollard. *Strategies: The Business of*

Being a Playwright in Canada. Toronto: The Playwright Union of Canada, 2000.

And look for regular updates of the following:
The Canadian Writer's Market. Toronto: McClelland & Stewart.
The Canadian Writers Guide: Official Handbook of the Canadian Authors Association. Markham, ON: Fitzhenry & Whiteside.
Novel & Short Story Writers' Market. Cincinnati: Writers' Digest Books.
The Writer's Handbook. The Writer, Inc.

MOTIVATION

Cameron, Julia. *The Artist's Way: A Spiritual Path to Higher Creativity.* New York: Jeremy P. Tarcher/Putnam, 1992. (Considered a bible by many writers!)

Oech, Roger von. *A Whack on the Side of the Head: How to Unlock Your Mind for Innovation.* New York: Warner Books, 1983.

Oech, Roger von. *A Kick in the Seat of the Pants: Using Your Explorer, Artist, Judge & Warrior to Be More Creative.* New York: Perennial Library (Harper & Row). Toronto: Fitzhenry & Whiteside, 1986.

Orenstein, Robert E. *The Mind Field.* New York: Grossman Publishers (The Viking Press), 1976.

Orenstein, Robert E. and David Sobel. *The Healing Brain: Breakthrough Discoveries About How the Brain Keeps Us Healthy.* New York: Simon & Schuster, 1987.

GRAMMAR & TEXTBOOKS

Chambers, J.K., ed. *Fitzhenry & Whiteside Canadian Thesaurus.* Markham, ON: Fitzhenry & Whiteside, 2001.

Clements, Warren, and J.A. McFarlane. *The Globe and Mail Style Book: A Guide to Language and Usage.* Toronto: McClelland & Stewart, 1998.

Follett, Wilson. *Modern American Usage: A Guide.* Ed. and completed by Jacques Barzun. New York: Hill & Wang, 1966.

Fowler, H.W. *A Dictionary of Modern English Usage.* Oxford at the Clarendon Press, 1957. (Ignore the new updated edition! It's not by Fowler and it's not as good.)

Gage Canadian Dictionary. Toronto: Gage Publishing, 1984.

Gordon, Karen Elizabeth. *The Well-Tempered Sentence: A Punctuation Handbook for the Innocent, the Eager, and the Doomed.* New Haven and New York: Ticknor & Fields, 1983.

Gordon, Karen Elizabeth. *The Transitive Vampire: A Handbook of Grammar for the Innocent, the Eager, and the Doomed.* New York: Times Books, 1984. (A combination of the two has been published.)

Partridge, Eric. *Origins: A Short Etymological Dictionary of Modern English.* New York: The Macmillan Company, 1959.

Roget, Peter Mark. *Roget's International Thesaurus.* New York: Thomas Y. Crowell Company, 1946.

Roget, Peter Mark and eds. The American Heritage Dictionary. *Roget's II The New Thesaurus.* Boston: Houghton Mifflin, 1980.

Strunk, William, Jr., and E. B. White. *The Elements of Style.* New York: Macmillan Publishing Co., Inc., 1972. (First published 1935, but it goes on forever.)

Tripp, Rhoda Thomas, compiler. *The International Thesaurus of Quotations.* New York: Perennial Library, Harper & Row, 1987.

Zinsser, William. *On Writing Well.* London, New York: Harper & Row, 1976. (The 25th anniversary edition is now available.)

The Canadian Encyclopedia Plus. (CD-ROM). Toronto: McClelland & Stewart, 1996.

SCREENWRITING

Breimer, Stephen F., Esq. *Clause by Clause.* New York: Bantam Doubleday Dell, 1995.

Cooper, Dona. *Writing Great Screenplays for Film and TV.* New York: Macmillan, 1994.

Field, Syd. *The Screenwriter's Guide to Hollywood.* New York: Dell Publishing, 1989.

Goldman, William. *Adventures in the Screen Trade.* New York: Jeremy P. Tarcher/Putnam, 1992. (This one is considered a bible by many writers!)

Goldman, William. *Which Lie Did I Tell?* New York: Pantheon Books, 2000.

Hauge, Michael. *How to Write and Sell Your Screenplay.* (Audiotape). Davenport Productions, Writer's Audioshop, 3 Casa Verde, Austin, TX 78734, 1989.

Herbert, Katherine Atwell. *Writing Scripts Hollywood Will Love: An Insider's Guide to Film and Television Scripts That Sell.* New York: Allworth Press, 1994.

Hunter, Lew. *Lew Hunter's Screenwriting 434.* New York: Putnam Publishing, a Perigee Book, 1993.

King, Viki. *How to Write a Movie in 21 Days: The Inner Movie Method.* New York: Harper & Row, Perennial Library, 1988.

Lee, Lance. *A Poetics for Screenwriters.* Austin: University of Austin Press, 2001.

McKee, Robert. *Story: Substance, Structure, Style, and the Principles of Screenwriting.* New York: Regan Books/HarperCollins, 1997.

Reichman, Rick. *Formatting Your Screenplay.* New York: Paragon House, 1992.

Roper, Carol. *How to Write a Screenplay in 9 Weeks.* (Audiotape). Writer's Consortium, P.O. Box 234112, Leucadia, CA 92023, 1994.

Serger, Linda. *The Art of Adaptation: Turning Fact and Fiction into Film.* New York: Henry Holt & Company, 1992.

Straczynski, J. Michael. *The Complete Book of Scriptwriting.* Cincinnati: Writers' Digest Books, 1982.

Swain, Dwight V. *Film Scriptwriting.* London, Boston: Focal Press, 1984.

Trottier, David. *The Screenwriter's Bible.* The Screenwriting Center, 2034 Lincoln Avenue, Suite 300, Anaheim, CA 92806, 1995.

Vogler, Christopher. *The Writer's Journey: Mythic Structure for Storytellers & Screenwriters.* Studio City, CA: Michael Wiese Productions, 1992.

THEATER

Brook, Peter. *The Empty Space.* London: MacGibbon & Kee, 1969.

Egri, Lajos. *The Art of Dramatic Writing.* New York: Simon & Schuster, 1960.

Johnstone, Keith. *Impro: Improvisation and the Theatre.* London: Faber & Faber, 1979.

Mamet, David. *3 Uses of the Knife: On the Nature and Purpose of Drama.* New York: The Columbia University Press, 1998.